D0431325

PRACTICING THE CHURCH YEAR

A SPIRITUALITY FOR THE HOME

COREAN BAKKE

Published by

Bakken Books

Acme, Washington

Copyright © 2011 by Corean Bakke

All rights reserved. No part of this publication, except those pages specifically mentioned below, may be reproduced, stored in a retrieval system, or transmitted, in any form or by any means, electronic, mechanical, photocopying, recording, or otherwise without the prior permission of Bakken Books.

The prayers on pages 151-183 may be reproduced.

Graham Maule/ WGRG copyright: WGRG/ Wild Goose Resource Group is a semi-autonomous project of the Iona Community, a charity registered in Scotland, No. SC003794.

BIBLICAL QUOTATIONS ARE TAKEN FROM:

The Bible: A New Translation by James Moffatt. Copyright © 1935 by Harper & Brothers. Copyright renewed 1962 by James A. R. Moffatt. Reprinted by permission of HarperCollins Publishers.

Contemporary English Version, copyright 1995, American Bible Society, New York, NY.

New Revised Standard Version Bible, copyright 1989, Division of Christian Education of the National Council of the Churches of Christ in the United States of America. Used by permission. All rights reserved.

Scripture quotations marked "NKJV™" are taken from the New King James Version®. Copyright © 1982 by Thomas Nelson, Inc. Used by permission. All rights reserved.

The Holy Bible Authorized King James Version: New York – Harper & Brothers Publishers.

PUBLISHED BY:
Bakken Books
PO Box 157
Acme, WA 98220
www.bakkenbooks.com

Fabric collage: Corean Bakke
Cover design: Greg Pearson
Illustrator: Woody Bakke

ISBN 13: 978-0-9755345-3-3
ISBN 10: 0-9755345-3-X

For Gina

But when the fullness of time had come

God sent his Son . . .

Galatians 4:4 NRSV

CONTENTS

ACKNOWLEDGEMENTS

Over the years, many professors dialogued with me about the church year as I took their courses. Their contributions to this book are intrinsic to its warp and weft.

Not until 18 April 2007 did I write to thank Robert Webber. My letter began:

> Twenty-two years ago, spring quarter of 1985, I took your class in early church history. It began my journey into the traditions of the church year . . .

He died a few days later on 27 April.

The dialogue with John Weborg continues. While I was a seminary student and he was professor of theology, pastoral care, and worship at North Park Theological Seminary in Chicago, I took every course he taught.

Tim Welch, organist/choirmaster at Immanuel Evangelical Lutheran Church when I was church homeless, invited and initiated me into the complexities of liturgical worship. The experience of singing in his choir was as demanding and fulfilling as enrolling in an extended course of study. After an intense four years – from the fifth Sunday of Lent 1996 to Pentecost Sunday 2000 – I suggested that a diploma would be in order.

Chris Berry, pastor and friend, supported this venturesome undertaking. Over cups of tea at the Shalom Center, he guided the shaping of this book and generously loaned books from his private library.

Lois Badgero, Gina Erickson, Elaine Bakke, Carol Cozad, Mary Carlson, Beve Minifie, Ruth Nelson, Joan Olson, and Karen MacKay reviewed and critiqued sections from the daily readings.

When the manuscript was presentable, readers representing a wide spread of church traditions responded with diverse and helpful suggestions. I owe many thanks to Kristin Carroccino, Kirk Reed, Bob Davies, Doug Haney, Jeannette Scholer, John Weborg, Dorothy Bass, Lois Badgero, and Jessica Bandstra.

Joan and Mark Olson tutored me by e-mail as I added website sources into the bibliography.

Joan Haner, a neighbor experienced in putting words on paper and critiquing books, enthusiastically accepted the task of proof reading an unknown subject. We spent many hours working at her kitchen table.

Woody Bakke, my son, drew the sketches for this book. He lives nearby in Oak Harbor where he is a special education teacher at the high school. He comes often to Bakken for a break from his intensive work with students.

My daughter-in-law, Andrea Bakke, gave me the gift of extended time by refusing to crowd production of this book into 2010. I am grateful for her strength and skills.

Greg Pearson, graphic designer, is a joy to work with. This cover is his fifth for Bakken Books.

I am blessed by having a husband with domestic skills. He prepared many dinners and cleaned up afterwards while this book took shape. I appreciate his patience with a task of unexpected duration. With his extensive library only a few steps away from my desk, books were always available for the taking without due dates.

INTRODUCTION

During my first year in seminary in Chicago, one blustery Sunday morning, I drove several hours to a tiny country church to supply preach. The congregation of thirty-nine people filled the sanctuary with harmony that would have shamed many mega-church choirs. We sang and prayed. They politely listened to the sermon I had struggled with all week. The coffee and cookies were magnificent.

Two things about that congregation have stuck with me for over thirty years. One defines the other. The congregation's *Weekly Activities and Announcements* were located after the collection of the offering, prior to the plates being brought forward to the chancel. I found that rather odd. When I asked the organist to explain that peculiar placement in the liturgy, she answered with a question. "Didn't you read the words above the back door when you left the church?" I honestly had not paid that much attention. I followed her up the rickety stairway from the basement to the sanctuary. Painted over the doors in huge letters, outlined in gold, were the words, "Worship is ended. Let the Service begin." These are words that I now find in many churches throughout my travels.

The people of this country church took "Service" seriously. The announcements were located in the liturgy as a reminder that all weekday activities were offerings of the people, an extension of worship on Sunday morning in the sanctuary. The congregation understood that they came to worship to be nourished and strengthened by the Word on Sunday so they could carry out their callings during the week in their community.

In *Practicing the Church Year: A Spirituality for the Home,* Corean Bakke has given the Church an insightful tool to assist us all in carrying out these callings. Corean has taken the *Ordo* – the rules governing how we celebrate the Church Year – out of the sacristy, out of the sanctuary, out of the pastors' offices, and placed it on the kitchen table. She invites the Church to continue the Service at home by stretching the velvet-lined box in which the currently accepted Church Year calendar resides.

Corean admits that she is "neither scholar nor an historian." For that we are grateful. She and her family have lived this kitchen-table spirituality and *Ordo* for years in her own home, which they have named Bakken. As an occasional guest at Bakken, I have been awestruck by the thought and detail that she brings to living out this spirituality. From the flowers and banners in the entry hall to the dishes used for meals, she makes practicing the Church Year meaningful, fun, and in many ways, mysterious.

In a culture where quality family time is relegated to carpools driving from ballet to soccer practice to swimming lessons to band to youth group, Corean has given us great excuse to take a break, to slow down, and to celebrate the presence of each other as the Spirit calls us together in our homes. It is, after all, from our homes that each day we go forth into the world, strengthened for Service.

I would be remiss if I did not offer a small word of warning. Corean has taken some liberties and shaken up some of the seasons of the Church Year with which we are so familiar. You know them – blue, white, green, purple, white, red, green. In doing so, she has turned the sometimes mundane into an exciting new rainbow of Spirituality. This is a rainbow not just of color, but also of new scripture readings and prayers that add a breath of fresh air to our spiritual lives.

If I ever leave the world of academia and campus ministry and return to parish ministry, I will strive to convince the people I serve to try this newly defined spirituality and *Ordo* not just in their homes but in the worship life of the congregation as well. As you use this guide, you will understand why.

Pass the coffee, please. Let us pray.

Rev. Christopher D. Berry
Campus Pastor
Western Washington University
Fall 2011

FOREWORD

A friend asked me to write about the church year. She wanted help in understanding what it meant and an explanation of the things I did in my home during the different seasons. She puzzled over my commitment to tradition.

Before responding, I searched through many books and websites for answers to my own lingering questions. Bits and pieces were scattered everywhere. I wanted to gather the important information into one place.

Having spent much time searching and preparing the answers, I recall the hide and seek game we children played during recess at the one-room country school I attended. Everyone hid while It, the person who would hunt, counted with eyes covered and then yelled, "Ready or not, here I come!"

I will never be completely ready to bring closure to this book, but the time to finish has come, whether I am ready or not.

I shall begin by establishing a personal context for this embrace of ancient tradition. The spirituality of the home I was born into, my earliest recollections of reaching out to God, my baptism, my education after high school, my marriage, and my church journey are all part of the story.

Although I am neither a scholar nor an historian, I will attempt a brief explanation of the church year calendar. This part *could* be dry, dusty, and dull to the point that you might be tempted to quit the book before you have hardly begun. I hope to make it timely and thought provoking. And I will describe observances of the church year found in churches that follow this calendar.

You will frequently encounter the term *liturgical church*. It is a church centered in worship that follows traditions of the historic church. Worship is guided by the liturgy: spoken and sung words involving a leader and the congregation in a continuous dialogue.

Over the years, as I became interested in maintaining a daily awareness of each season, an organizing principle emerged: a spirituality rooted in the church year. I will describe practices developed for each season in my home.

The church year is a story grounded in ancient time and place, repeated every year. The seasons – Advent, Christmas, Epiphany, Lent, Easter, and Pentecost – are like chapters in the story.

Daily readings and prayers for the seasons, a significant practice that deserves its own division of the book, are together at the end. The illustrator for this book, my son Woody, drew freehand and approximate maps, lettering in the names of essential landmarks and specific sites included in the daily readings.

This book is my explanation of the story embodied in the church year and the description of making it relevant for contemporary time and place.

Corean Bakke
Pentecost Season 2011

PART I

JOURNEY OF DISCOVERY

My parents joined *Cor* from my father's name with *ean* from my mother's name to make a name for their first-born child. Cornelius John Jantz was born in South Dakota into a rural German Dutch Mennonite home. Jean MacKay Foote was born in Minnesota into an urban Scotch English Presbyterian home. Both families were directly descended from immigrants to this country.

Cornelius and Jean married during the Great Depression. They wanted to go as foreign missionaries to Africa. My father's oldest brother and two sisters had already gone. When "the Lord shut the door" – as my mother explained – they instead became home missionaries with the American Sunday School Union and were sent to Lewistown, Montana.

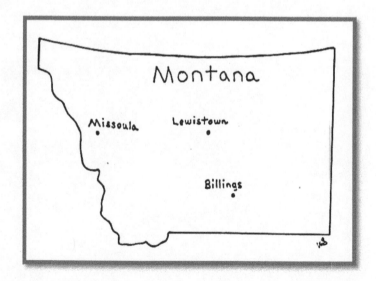

My father bought a plot of land at 311 East Lake Avenue in Lewistown where he built a tiny two-story house.

From there he drove out into ranch country to organize Sunday schools where no local church existed. Those Sunday schools met in any building available, often in the schoolhouse. Men, women, and children fitted themselves into school desks with attached seats. Songs were sung and the lessons began. On the Sundays when my father came to be with them, a preaching service was added. Those gatherings were strictly non-denominational and most people were unaware of my parents' home church affiliations.

I have no memory of the music in those rural places of Montana apart from standing on a chair, so I could be seen, and singing:

> O who can make a flower?
> I'm sure I can't. Can you?
> O who can make a flower?
> No one but God tis true.

That little song had many verses. My mother coached me from her seat in the front row by holding up a symbol for each verse.

My father traveled long distances to keep in touch with his Sunday schools, sometimes over a hundred miles in one direction. In winter he contended with snow and intense cold and when warmth returned, muddy roads mired his tires. He often left Lewistown on Friday or Saturday and stayed overnight with ranchers in those sparse communities. During such times, I was allowed to walk by myself to First Baptist Church in Lewistown. The robed choir, pipe organ, and hymnals introduced me to church music. I assumed that their way was the proper way to worship.

As a small child I was very impressionable and drawn to doing the right thing. In my heart I desired to please God.

I remember sitting at the top of the stairs with my mother, listening to her read from the thick Bible storybook and praying before I crawled into bed. There likely was a time when my mother asked whether I wanted to invite Jesus into my heart. I would have wanted to do that.

Every morning at the breakfast table, before we ate, my father read from the Bible and then prayed. I have no memories of any of the passages read. It was a sacred ritual at the beginning of each day. Lunch and supper were likewise begun with prayer, usually a memorized prayer that we recited together.

Music was fun for me. I began piano lessons at age five with a teacher who rode her bicycle to our home. In third grade I enthusiastically learned to sight-read singing *Solfège* (*do, re, mi, fa, sol, la, ti, do*). Soon I was playing out of my mother's Presbyterian hymnal.

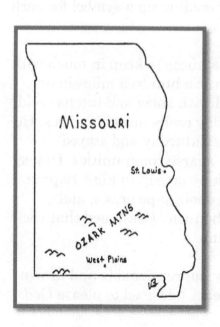

When I was eight years old, my father requested a transfer to a warmer, more populous area. We moved to the Ozarks of southern Missouri. No distance was beyond reach on a Sunday morning. Our entire family accompanied my father to the Sunday schools under his supervision. His Sunday schedule evolved into a regular preaching circuit. Again, as before, these were non-denominational gatherings.

Rural gospel singing in the Ozarks bore no resemblance to any other music I had encountered. Shaped-note hymnals were filled with songs and hymns mostly new to me, written in a strange style and notation. Confronted and puzzled by the music, I neither cared for the way it sounded nor for the informality that accompanied it. Resistance overpowered curiosity. From the beginning, I started off on the wrong foot in rural Ozark culture, wishing I was not there.

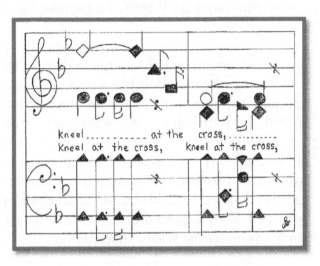

I looked forward to vacations when we left the Ozarks behind. Even as a child traveling with my parents, the prospect of attending church – especially in a big city – excited me. The building, formality, and furnishings gave me much to look at during worship. Music was the primary attraction: preludes and postludes played on pipe organs, congregational music sung out of thick hymnals (with round notes), and robed choirs of men and women. This combination of music included within a one-hour worship service was like water on dry land. I soaked it up and thirsted for more.

In my teen years, I heard people say that if you cannot remember having invited Jesus into your heart, you are not a Christian. That put me in a confusing dilemma. I had no vivid memory of extending that invitation. For years I struggled with my spiritual identity. It finally resolved when I made an intellectual decision to take all the necessary steps – which by then included repentance – and became a Christian. All the bases were covered. I would not worry anymore. However, I still did not have an answer ready for people who expected a specific memory and date of a born-again experience.

In addition to organizing Sunday schools, my father organized vacation Bible schools during the months of June and July and concluded his summer schedule with Bible camps. One summer during my high school years, my father included a baptismal service for youth from the rural Sunday schools who had become Christians. It took place at the Hammond's Mill Camp, seventeen miles from West Plains, Missouri. Barefoot and wearing a sleeveless blouse and gathered skirt, I walked into the Jacks Fork River and was baptized, keeping my distance from the swift current and a wary eye alert for water moccasins.

☙ ☙ ☙

Mennonite influences predominated in our family. As a young girl I was not allowed to cut my hair or wear shorts or pants. I always had to wear a dress, even when playing outside. As a teenager, my desire to wear lipstick created a family crisis. I was to *look* like a Christian. Movies and dancing were not allowed and plays were suspect.

Sunday afternoon and evening pastimes were markedly different from the rest of the week. It was the Lord's Day and not to be desecrated by secular activities. We would not think of going shopping. That was done on Saturday. When, as a high school student, I sometimes did homework on Sunday, it was with a deep sense of guilt.

With no relatives nearby, we mainly socialized with other families involved in non-denominational mission work, both foreign and home missions.

My mother liked biblical art and had reproductions framed and hung in our home. Her favorite showed Mary Magdalene weeping at the tomb on Easter morning. An elegantly lettered and framed quote hung above my mother's Seth Thomas clock that chimed every quarter hour.

"Only one life, t'will soon be past;
Only what's done for Christ will last."

– attributed to David Livingstone

During high school I began attending First Baptist Church in West Plains, a Southern Baptist church. Although my parents did not allow me to join that church, people treated me as though I were a member. They asked whether I would be interested in organ lessons and paid for them. I occasionally played for Sunday evening services to give their organist some time off. In 1956 when each high school graduate in the youth group received a copy of the newly published Revised Standard Version, the congregation graciously included me. My father did not trust that translation and warned me to use it sparingly. He used the King James Scofield Reference Bible exclusively.

With high school finished, I looked forward to leaving the Ozarks.

My parents wanted me to go to a Bible school to establish my faith before going to college. When I filled out the entrance application for Moody Bible Institute in Chicago, one question asked for my church affiliation. Since I was not a member of any church, my mother was concerned that a straight answer might jeopardize my acceptance. She instructed me to reply that I planned to join Moody Church[1] in Chicago. I was the only Moody student among the new member candidates when I became a church member for the first time. On Sunday mornings I attended worship with hundreds of other students, all of us walking the mile from school to church on LaSalle Boulevard. The sanctuary in that vast historic church seats nearly 4000 people.

At that time, Moody was a three-year school. Students chose a major from the available study tracks and received a diploma at graduation. I chose the Sacred Music Course. The music department had evolved a course of study that paralleled studies at a conservatory of music with hymnody added. Gospel songs – energetic rhythmic verses followed by easy to remember refrains – were included in that broad category. As a piano student I was expected to become proficient at improvising accompaniments for gospel songs and hymns, and strongly encouraged to learn the art of arranging them into solos for piano. Perhaps because of my eight years in the Ozarks, where I closed my ears to the music around me, I had little interest in spending time with gospel music. With continuous piano lessons all through grade school and high school, I arrived at Moody proficient in reading music but wanting in aural musical skills. Improvising was out of reach.

---

[1] Moody Church and Moody Bible Institute, named for Dwight L. Moody, are separate institutions, connected only by name.

I met Ray Bakke a month into the first semester. We were assigned to the same ministry team and rode the subway each week to the Pacific Garden Mission. Our role was to provide music for the service that preceded the evening meal for homeless men. Ray was also a first-year student, enrolled in the Missions Course. This venture into a city during our late teen-age years became a critical time for examining beliefs and values. We spent many hours discussing our backgrounds as we got acquainted. For Ray, who never failed to read a daily newspaper, it was a time of expanding his rural experience to include the wonders of a big city. For me, it was a time of adjusting to daily life on an urban campus of one city block, wondering what my future would involve.

☻ ☻ ☻

After graduation from Moody Bible Institute and one year of college, Ray and I married and began life together in Seattle where he was youth and music director at Elim Baptist Church. When the pastor left, Ray became interim pastor. He then went to a sister church, Dunlap Baptist, while he finished his degree at Seattle Pacific University, as it is now called. Two sons were born during these years.

In 1965 we moved to Chicago for access to the seminary of choice for my husband's next academic pursuit: Trinity Evangelical Divinity School in nearby Deerfield. He became youth director at Edgewater Baptist Church, and then pastor of Fairfield Avenue Baptist Church. My mother no longer had reason to be concerned about my church affiliation as I now had a four-fold increase in church membership since enrolling at Moody Bible Institute.

In 1966 I returned to Moody as a part-time instructor in piano and continued my studies at Chicago Musical College, completing a bachelor's and master's degree in piano performance. My teaching position at Moody expanded into a full-time appointment to the music faculty. Gospel music and informality in worship continued in both my worship life and my professional life.

At Fairfield Avenue Baptist Church I experienced regular, once a month communion. This ritual made me increasingly uncomfortable. The solemn decorum of pastor and deacons and the selection of hymns such as "There is a Fountain Filled With Blood" created an on-going dilemma. When my children outgrew the nursery and sat beside me in the worship services, my discomfort included their exclusion. Baptists did not allow children to participate in communion until they publicly professed their faith in Jesus and were baptized.

Music had been a big part of my life from my earliest memories, but my usefulness as a pianist had limits. All solo piano music was expected to remind the listeners of familiar hymns and gospel songs. Because I was not skilled at improvisation and did not enjoy published hymn arrangements, my solo contributions to the worship were few. No place existed for the classical music I could easily have played.

When I became interested in introducing other art forms into worship and encouraged a dancer – a member of the young adult group at the church – to interpret the reading of a psalm, the matter went to the deacon board for discussion. The founding members of this church read their King James Bibles as my parents did. Psalm 150 was not to be taken literally:

Praise ye the Lord. Praise God in his sanctuary:
 praise him in the firmament of his power.
Praise him for his mighty acts:
 praise him according to his excellent greatness.
Praise him with the sound of the trumpet:
 praise him with the psaltery and harp.
Praise him with the timbrel and dance . . .

We were not to praise the Lord with *dancing*. It was as though the word had been crossed out (replaced with *sitting?*). I had pushed too hard against their theological and cultural barriers.

☉ ☉ ☉

After pastoring at Fairfield Baptist for ten years, my husband resigned and became a seminary professor. For the first time, our family had freedom about where to attend church. After months of searching we gave up trying to make a single choice. Ray joined a church affiliated with Northern Baptist Theological Seminary where he was teaching. He told our three teenage sons – Woody, Brian, and our adopted son also named Brian – that they could decide where they wanted to go. They returned to the church we had just left. I eagerly applied that decision to myself. For twenty years – since my marriage – I had been Baptist. Now I longed to be something else and began a list of what I wanted in a church:

 Walking distance
 Ethnic mix
 Pipe organ
 Liturgy
 Architecture
 Opportunity

Good preaching and good music were not on the list. They would have complicated the list beyond possibility, especially within walking distance. I was married to a good preacher. In the previous churches I always had to adjust to whatever the music was and compensate with musical experiences outside the church. I would try to do that again.

"Walking distance" as number one on my list related to our being a one-car family. Now that Ray was no longer officially pastoring, he would likely receive numerous invitations to preach. I rode public transportation to my teaching job at Moody four days every week and did not want to ride it on Sunday as well.

I joined Epworth United Methodist Church, eight blocks from my Chicago home. For years, I had admired this striking stone church but had never stepped inside. As I walked up the wide steps to the entrance for the first time, music from the pipe organ greeted me, played by a Filipino youth. Many Filipinos were scattered throughout the congregation. It had a modest liturgy printed in the bulletin. Empty pews signified opportunity. It fulfilled everything on my list. An African-American woman and I joined Epworth on 30 March 1980.

Joining this church was an idealistically driven decision. I admired John Wesley and his transformation of urban peoples. Epworth was located in a once grand neighborhood now fallen on hard times. I saw it as a place where I could get busy and make a difference. And not least, the pastor was a woman. Women-in-ministry was a controversial topic where I worked.

Not until becoming Methodist did I learn that color conveys meaning. I learned about paraments, the special cloth coverings used on pulpit, lectern, and communion table. My first volunteer job was to arrive in time to go to the sacristy, remove the correct cloth from its tissue-paper wrapper, and place it on the communion table. At the end of the service I returned it to the sacristy. The pulpit and lectern paraments remained in place.

At Epworth I learned about the seasons of the church year and why the correct communion cloth was so important. Each season had a name with a special meaning, but as soon as I left the church, that information left my mind. It had no relevance or meaning for me during the week. Each Sunday, on my walk to church, I would try to remember.

Epworth is where I experienced an alternative method of communion. It was called *eucharist*, a Greek word meaning *thanksgiving*. Instead of sitting in the pews, we walked up to the communion rail and knelt down. Instead of passing trays with tiny broken particles of soda crackers, clumps of bread were broken from a loaf and placed in our hands. Instead of heavy trays filled with miniature portions of grape juice, we all drank from a large chalice. Instead of somberness, we felt companionship in kneeling beside each other. Mirth meshed with thanksgiving. On one occasion the assistant to the pastor became self-conscious about her wide neckline when she bent over. Laughter came precariously near the surface for me when she approached, clutching her neckline together with one hand while extending the chalice in the other.

Epworth is where I learned and participated in early efforts by Chicago churches to provide overnight shelters for homeless men and women. On a sub-freezing night, knowing that this would soon be an agenda at my church, Ray drove me with my sleeping bag to a nearby shelter. I selected an unoccupied space on the floor and bedded down. When Epworth opened a shelter for men in the gymnasium, I took my turn keeping watch through the night in company with a friend.

In retrospect, it was good that I had few responsibilities during the fifteen years at Epworth United Methodist Church (1980-1995). I traveled internationally with my husband and opened myself to music and the arts in every country we visited. Each autumn it became more difficult to return to my teaching position in the music department at Moody Bible Institute where *world music* was not yet considered important and not included in any of the classes. My world had opened wide. I became eager to learn, participate, and teach in broader areas than the school offered.[2]

☺ ☺ ☺

The discovery of a degree in theology and the arts caught my attention, but the program was offered only in California. I lived in Illinois. Moreover, my husband and I now had three teenagers about to graduate from high school

---

[2] The conversion of my ears began when a student asked to play a rag. The discovery of American folk music prepared me for folk music around the world and for inviting an Ozark quartet to sing "Farther Along" (from the shaped-note hymnal) at my father's funeral. He had requested it.

and enter college. How could I possibly become a student at such a time?

An unexpected opportunity surfaced. Spouses of professors at Northern Baptist Theological Seminary could enroll tuition free. The Association of Chicago Theological Schools (ACTS), organized in 1984, published a catalog of classes offered by twelve theological seminaries in the Chicago area, including the seminary where Ray was professor. Students could cross-register into any of them. My husband suggested that I design a course in theology and the arts by choosing from the classes described in the new catalog. I resigned my teaching position and became a student again in 1984.

A class in early church history transformed my life. Robert Webber (a recent convert to the Episcopal church) taught each class session from the same perspective: the Christ Event, symbolized by the small cross he drew in the upper left-hand corner of the chalkboard. During each class, he filled the expansive chalkboard from top to bottom. As he lectured, the church year unfolded as a historical way of remembering. I had never before encountered the traditions. They made so much sense. How had such an amazing organization of the faith evaded me for so long? I sat in the front row, absorbing this marvelous revelation.

At Catholic Theological Union (CTU) on Chicago's south side, I enrolled in "Liturgical Seasons." I asked my Methodist pastor to suggest a season that I might use for my class project. He (the new pastor) suggested Pentecost. It was the most difficult season for him because resources for the seasons of the church year ran out of ideas after Pentecost Sunday. Often only a mere half page was devoted to the following six months! He suggested I plan something for that barren time in the church year. He would gladly use it at Epworth.

My project was titled: "Sundays After Pentecost: What To Do With the Last Half of the Church Year." Four of us formed a committee to develop a congregational response for twenty-five consecutive weeks: June 1 through November 16. Members of the congregation chose one of the gospel readings from the lectionary to read in the service, and then interpreted it with expressions of their own creativity. People were reluctant to plan alternate activities on Sunday mornings that summer because of what they would miss. Sundays following the Day of Pentecost in 1986 were not barren.

A favorite response involved Luke 13:22-30. The Narrow Door. Two sisters, excellent photographers and well-traveled, put together a slide show to illustrate the reading. They painted red an unusually narrow door leading into the church from the alley and took a photo for that day's interpretation of the gospel reading.

My professor at CTU was not impressed. For Catholics, Sundays following Pentecost were filled with saints to be commemorated. But Methodists did not follow the sanctoral calendar, filled with dates for commemorating saints. He was a scholar. I was a novice searching for a way through new territory. The class came to an end with no resolution of our impasse.

☉ ☉ ☉

I took advantage of the cross-registration opportunities and enrolled in every class related to the church year. What had begun as a short-term course of study extended to include

a Master of Arts in Theological Studies (MATS) in 1985,
a Master of Divinity (M.Div.) equivalency in 1988, and a
Doctor of Ministry (D.Min.) in 1990.

☺ ☺ ☺

For fifteen years I looked for opportunities to make
myself useful at Epworth in ways that did not involve my
special interests and abilities. Worship was off limits because
the pastors (four different ones during those years) worked
without worship committees. The organist/choir director also
worked independently.

An uncontested area of worship at this church became
space for me to explore and develop. Banners. These cloth
hangings are large and colorful and help identify each of the
seasons of the church year. Past efforts were haphazardly
stored in the sacristy. After doing an inventory, I suggested
new projects. A large blank wall over the choir balcony at the
front of the sanctuary offered potential for visual statements
of the seasons.

For Lent, a small team of us made a cityscape of black
cloth – with recognizable Chicago architectural landmarks –
and mounted it on the wall. Lettering across the top read:
"Lord, have mercy." Street and gang violence penetrated the
city, even the very neighborhood surrounding the church. For
Pentecost, we made red, orange, and yellow flames of fire for
that wall.

At Easter we made twin banners of white with gold
lamé lettering – "Christ is Risen" "He is Risen Indeed" – and
hung them on either side of the choir balcony. For Epiphany
we made mini-banners based on the gospel readings and hung
them across the dark wooden paneling that framed the
platform.

To replace a decrepit Pentecost pulpit hanging, I made a new red parament using an African design: flames of fire touching down on black heads. With mother-of-pearl buttons I framed the design as an arch-shaped window.

My Methodist identity came to an end when the pastoral ministry of the church narrowed to a single issue: to successfully guide the church through steps to become a Reconciling Congregation and to adopt a public statement welcoming and affirming gays and lesbians. Discussions continued for months. I had recently completed a ten-week class devoted entirely to homosexuality. My personal turmoil left me exhausted with no energy for new discussions on the same topic. Our time in Chicago was limited. Ray and I had purchased property in Washington State and were planning to relocate where he grew up. Before leaving Chicago I wanted to find another church where I could immerse myself in church music and worship planning. The struggle at Epworth provided that opportune time. I resigned my membership in November of 1995.

☺ ☺ ☺

During my ensuing church-homeless period, I attended the community Thanksgiving service near my home. Choirs from many churches sang but it was a Lutheran choir that drew my attention. If I were to choose a church within walking distance, with excellent music and opportunities for me to be involved, I should become Lutheran. In March, on the fifth Sunday of Lent, I became a member of Immanuel Evangelical Lutheran Church on Chicago's north side.

This final choice of church identity intensified my involvement with the church year. I joined the worship committee of life-long Lutherans. We met regularly and exuberantly planned each season. I joined the choir. That commitment involved an intensive two-hour rehearsal on Thursday evenings, a twenty-minute warm-up on Sunday mornings, and participation in all of the services.

The music was more than I had dared hope for and existed within walking distance of my house! Learning to follow the Lutheran liturgy felt like going to school again. The intense combination of choir and worship – four hours each week – speedily propelled my liturgical education forward. No longer was I trying to remember the name of the season and what it meant on my walk to church.

☺ ☻ ☻

I was a new Lutheran of only eight days when Holy Week of 1996 began. As a member of the choir, I had much to learn. Maundy Thursday, Good Friday, and the Great Vigil of Easter were planned as a continuous three-part worship service leading into Easter. A spiral-bound booklet titled "The Three Days" contained fifty-five pages of liturgy, hymns, instructions, sidebars of explanatory notes, and graphic art prepared by the energetic and talented worship committee. Information on the beginning page of the liturgy read:

> Tonight begins a very long church
> service. So long that it takes three days! These
> three days are called the Triduum, and are the
> most important days of the year for a
> Christian.

For Maundy Thursday (from *mandatum* meaning *commandment*) the evening liturgy was a reminder of Jesus' new commandment to love one another.

> I am giving you a new command. You
> must love each other, just as I have loved
> you. If you love each other, everyone will
> know that you are my disciples.
>
> John 13:34-35 CEV

The liturgy continued with a ritual washing of feet.

> During the meal Jesus got up, removed
> his outer garment, and wrapped a towel
> around his waist. He put some water into
> a large bowl. Then he began washing his
> disciples' feet and drying them with the
> towel he was wearing.
>
> John 13:4-5 CEV

At the conclusion of the Maundy Thursday liturgy, the altar was stripped as the congregation watched and listened to Psalm 22 sung in darkness. Everyone silently left the church.

Good Friday's observance continued the next evening. A single reader read the Passion Story from John's Gospel in segments, followed by alternating musical responses sung by the congregation and by the *a cappella* quartet singing in the rear balcony. After each reading, a candle was extinguished. When all eight candles were extinguished and the reading finished, a procession carried a rough-hewn cross into the dimly lighted church. Prayers and adoration of the cross were followed by silence.

The Great Vigil of Easter began outdoors at 10:00 p.m. on the church lawn where a new fire was created with sparks in order to light the large new *Paschal* candle. The congregation stood watching and singing as the pastor ceremoniously inscribed the candle with a cross, the year, *alpha* and *omega,* and five studs of incense to represent the five wounds of Christ. The lighted candle led the congregation into the dark church as a symbol of Christ's resurrection and victory over sin and darkness.

As the cantor sang the *Exsultet,* a lengthy Easter proclamation, we lighted our candles from the *Paschal* candle. The night progressed with seven readings, each followed by a choral response, silence, and prayer. The baptismal liturgy followed.

Finally, at midnight, the announcement came:

Alleluia! Christ is risen!

The congregation responded:

He is risen indeed! Alleluia!

A fanfare played by brass instruments in the rear balcony began the Resurrection Eucharist. This celebration of the resurrection – without a sermon – concluded the continuous liturgy of the Three Days. The worship booklet ended with a practical reminder:

> The joyful celebration of our Lord's
> Resurrection continues tomorrow morning
> with the Holy Eucharist at 10:30 a.m. Set
> your clocks forward one hour tonight.

A champagne reception followed!

When darkness turned to the light of day the congregation gathered at the usual Sunday morning time. The new worship folder for that morning was simply titled "Easter." It contained sixteen pages of liturgy.

That Easter experience contrasted with *all* prior Easters of my life. It had always seemed inappropriate to me that Christmas celebrations took more preparation and time than Easter. Christmas had worn me down year after year while Easter, in comparison, was nearly effortless. Preparation, time, and energy-expended finally fit the celebration of this most important festival of my faith.

Four years later, in 2000, at the conclusion of Pentecost Sunday worship and fellowship hour at Immanuel Evangelical Lutheran Church, my husband and I began the two thousand mile drive to Acme, the rural community in northwest Washington State where he grew up.

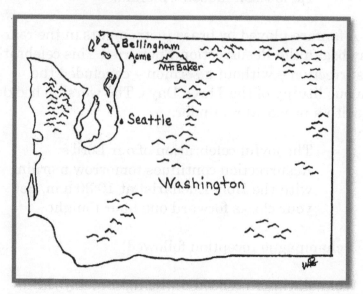

Acme is a village with a self-appointed mayor. The business district includes a general store and café on one side of the highway, faced by the post office, the headquarters for Whatcom County Fire District #16, and Acme Presbyterian Church on the other side. Acme Elementary School is off on a side street. In 1992 we purchased acreage one and a half miles south of Acme. Each July following found us living and working on the undeveloped property.

On Sundays we explored worship options for our eventual move to this community. Besides visiting Acme Presbyterian, we drove to churches north and south looking for a Lutheran possibility for me. Ray's church home identity would remain in Chicago. It was less important for him to find a local congregation since he would often be away filling pulpits on Sundays. Finally Ray made the decision: we would worship with our neighbors in the Acme Presbyterian Church. On special feast days we would drive into Bellingham and attend St. Paul's Episcopal Church.

This was my first experience of a Presbyterian church. Worship was similar to my Baptist experience where the sermon was the climax of each service. Communion was added once a month. Each Sunday recalled the informality of worship in the Ozarks.

Then 9/11 happened, that spectacularly monstrous feat of evil.

Ray and I attended a prayer service that evening led by pastors of the small rural churches around us. As the week progressed, a hunger grew within me to participate in liturgy and ritual that defined my beliefs: to sing "Lord, have mercy," to remember the baptismal vow renouncing all the forces of evil and the devil, to recite the Apostles' Creed, to kneel and hear the words, "This is the body of Christ broken for you." I told Ray of my plans to drive into Bellingham for worship on Sunday. That was the beginning of my regular attendance at Our Saviour's Lutheran Church.

The worship experience at Acme Presbyterian resulted in lasting friendships with our neighbors, a significant happening for my first year in a new community. That experience also confirmed my preference for Lutheran liturgy and hymnals. On the last Sunday of Epiphany 2002 I joined Our Saviour's Lutheran Church in Bellingham.

☙ ☙ ☙

Advent is a colorful season at Our Saviour's. The blue paraments – including drop cloths on lectern and pulpit plus the long altar cloth that drapes over the table – are my favorite set of fabric art at this church. Each Sunday of Advent a large fabric candle is attached to the wall behind the altar-table, each in a different vibrant jewel color, until four of them in graduating sizes complete the set. Each Sunday during the *Meal* part of our worship, colors and symbols of the cloth art greet every person who walks forward to receive the bread and wine. The Advent wreath, with four candles surrounding the larger Christ candle in the center, is placed on a stand. A Christmas tree is put up during Advent, decorated with blue and white ornaments.

Choir and congregational music for all four Sundays of Advent avoids Christmas carols. A major part of our waiting during this season involves waiting for Christmas music. The carols begin on Christmas Eve with a choir concert followed by a worship service, both of them filled with carols. With a bell choir now part of the seasonal traditions, the service draws to a close with the bells playing "Silent Night" in the darkened church as each person lights a candle. The organ leads the singing of that carol to conclude the service.

The crèche appears during Advent as we wait. Figures are added as the readings introduce them. On Christmas Eve the Christ Child is included. The Magi are still on their way and may be found in a small hallway leading to the narthex, the space immediately inside the front doors of the church.

Epiphany has the Magi arriving at the crèche. After this, the crèche disappears for another year. Light is celebrated during this time, beginning with the star that guided the Magi from the East to Bethlehem, and ending with the intense light of the Transfiguration on the last Sunday in Epiphany.

During Lent at Our Saviour's we observe rituals of restraint and repentance. Some churches have no alleluias, no bells, no passing of the peace, and no postludes. Our Saviour's is not that strict, but the alleluias – ALLELUIA lettered on paper – are ceremoniously placed in a covered wooden box, not to appear again until Easter morning. Wednesday evenings of Lent are traditionally times of gathering for a simple meal of soup and bread and working through a Lenten study as preparation for Easter.

Holy Week is launched with Palm/Passion Sunday, a service of double focus. Palm branches are distributed in the narthex as people gather. The service begins there and processes into the sanctuary on the first hymn. It then becomes a Passion observance as the extended story from John's Gospel is read dramatically. One year the readings were done in costume, enhancing the drama of the story.

Maundy Thursday and Good Friday are observed in the evenings. Easter Vigil is optional in this church, a practical consideration for the aging congregation.

Easter Sunday morning begins with breakfast and time to decorate a large wooden cross with fresh flowers. It will be placed in the sanctuary as the service begins. The liturgy is carefully chosen and printed in the worship folders. The choir sings multiple times beginning with an introit from the rear of the center aisle. Hand bells play from the balcony. The post-communion canticle, written by the organist/choir director, is sung for each Sunday of Easter. The Easter recessional is often my hymn, "At Dawn They Came," sung with tambourines played by both adults and children.

Pentecost Sunday is celebrated with red paraments in place. The pastor wears an exquisite red stole of liturgical art bearing symbols of the day: dove and flames of fire. The congregation arrives in red apparel to find red geraniums in small pots outlining the entire width of the platform. During the following week God's Gardeners, a group of volunteers, plant these flowers in the church gardens. Bilingual members of the congregation may participate by reading scripture in their mother tongue to commemorate the birth of the Church, now present in most countries of the world.

The next Sunday the sanctuary is attired in white to observe Trinity Sunday. The following Sunday begins the long stretch of green. It will prevail until Advent begins in late November, except when interrupted for a Sunday here and there when minor festivals require a different color. Our Saviour's Lutheran Church identifies this time as *Sundays following Pentecost.* Other churches – including Roman Catholic, Episcopal, and most Presbyterian churches – identify this time as *Ordinary Time.*

Reformation Sunday, at the end of October, is what I call an elevated minor festival in the Lutheran church. Red paraments appear for this celebration in honor of Martin Luther's leadership and discovery that "The just shall live by faith."[3] The new hymnal, *Evangelical Lutheran Worship,* has nineteen hymns authored or composed by Martin Luther. The

---

[3] Romans 1:17 KJV

34

congregation arrives wearing red shirts, ties, sweaters, jackets, sweatshirts, and suspenders.

The Sunday following Reformation involves another change of color: white for All Saints' Day. Names of departed church and family members are read from different locations in the sanctuary. Between readers, a selected combination of hand bells are rung in remembrance of those loved ones.

Christ the King Sunday, five Sundays before Christmas, marks the end of the church year. The church attire changes from green to white. This is followed by the first Sunday of Advent, the beginning of the new church year.

☙ ☙ ☙

Not until landing in a liturgical church did I realize the discrepancies between the civic calendar and the church year calendar. Apart from Christmas and Easter, holidays and other special days on the civic calendar – New Year's Eve and New Year's Day, Valentine's Day, President's Day, Mothers' Day and Fathers' Day, Memorial Day, Independence Day, Labor Day, Halloween, and Thanksgiving – do not appear on the church year calendar.

When I decided to follow the church year and celebrate major festivals of that calendar in my home, the problem arose: how would I relate to civic celebrations and family celebrations of birthdays, anniversaries, and graduations? The church calendar had a ready solution. It includes *minor* festivals. I would adapt the category of minor festivals to include other days in my home as needed. The Church observes both major and minor festivals. I would do likewise.

This has a practical dimension. When my ever-traveling husband must be away from home on a day when a personal response is expected from him, he can breathe easily. He knows that I will regard it either as a minor festival and excuse him, or as a moveable feast and reschedule the celebration.

My nearest neighbor has a passion for year-round outdoor decorating. Her Christmas display includes an actual shed with large standing rag-dolls clothed as Joseph and Mary and the shepherds. I often wonder how they survive in the constant rain we normally have in December. That is her most elaborate decoration. Other civic calendar dates are observed more modestly, but always remembered. I invited her, wondering whether she would notice *my* decorations. On her first visit to my home, other things caught her attention and dominated our conversation.

The only guests who recognize the meaning of my seasonal decorations are those who worship in liturgical churches. My spirituality does not speak to non-liturgical guests. It is a foreign language to them.

But that is not a deterrent. The church year invited me to live in the story. The entire year became, for me, time within seasons focused on a distinctive call and response. Dressing the house for each season has become a meaningful tradition in our home and an important practice of my spirituality.

PART II

A PRIMER ON THE CHURCH YEAR

The church calendar that is now followed evolved over many centuries. Jesus' first followers observed their Jewish traditions even as they cultivated Christian traditions. Observances continue to change. This is disconcerting to anyone looking for absoluteness, but welcoming to anyone hoping for flexibility and creativity.

Jesus was Jewish. His earliest followers were Jewish. The last day of the week, the Sabbath, was the most important day of the Jewish week. It was a day of rest – in memory of God's resting upon completing creation of the world – and freedom from all labor. Food for that day had to be prepared in advance. The Sabbath began at sunset on the eve of the sixth day, when the mother in the home lighted the candles.

The first day of the week, the day when Jesus rose from death, became sacred to his followers. They gave it a special name: The Lord's Day. His resurrection on the first day of the week gave it greater importance. It became a day of worship and celebration.

Whereas the Sabbath was a family observance, the Lord's Supper was not a private family observance. When Jesus ritualized bread and wine and asked that such a meal be observed to remember his sacrifice, his disciples surrounded him. Gatherings of followers likely met in homes following the resurrection to worship and observe the Lord's Supper.

Rituals in the homes of Jesus' followers, after his crucifixion, resurrection, and ascension, included both Jewish and Christian observances.

As the person responsible for feeding people in my home, I notice the many touch-points between food and faith. Passover, the hurried meal in Egypt while awaiting notice to begin the long trek to the Promised Land, is still a central feast in Judaism. Jesus introduced a mystical meal to his followers on the evening of his betrayal and arrest. That meal, the Lord's Supper, has occurred repeatedly for over two thousand years in all parts of the world.

SUNDAY

The first day of the week – Day of the Sun in the Roman calendar – was established as the Christian day of worship when Constantine became emperor.[4] In 321 A.D. he decreed that Sunday would become the official day of rest for the empire. Christians were then able to worship freely and plan their day accordingly.

Sunday worship moved from hiding places, caves, and homes to specially constructed buildings as Christianity gained official recognition. With safe places for worship, attention could be given to formalizing and beautifying the worship environment.

---

[4] Frank Senn, *Christian Liturgy: Catholic and Evangelical* (Minneapolis: Fortress Press, 1997), 87.

MAJOR FEAST DAYS

EASTER

The Nicene Council, in 325 AD, decreed that the process for selecting the most authentic Sunday of the year for celebrating the resurrection would follow two steps. First, the spring equinox must occur, when daytime and nighttime are the same length. Then a full moon must occur. Those essential factors may come together on any date between March 22 and April 25. The Sunday following would be as close as possible to the actual anniversary of the Resurrection of our Lord.

Easter is called a moveable feast. Every year the date must be calculated anew. This primary festival of the Church and its most important celebration is a continually changing date in the civic calendar

Easter, the name given to this most special of all Sundays in the year, could be an adaptation of the name *Ēostre,* a Teutonic goddess of spring. When that name was given is uncertain.

PENTECOST

Pentecost means fifty. Fifty days after Passover marked an important Jewish festival celebrating the conclusion of the spring reaping season. Jesus chose that day to fulfill the promise made to his followers. On the Day of Pentecost the Holy Spirit descended on them, energizing and emboldening. This happening caught the attention of on-lookers in Jerusalem and is remembered as the birth of the Church.[5]

---

[5] Acts 2:1-13

It is likely that the early followers of Jesus continued celebrating important Jewish festivals, including Pentecost. When that day became more significant for them as a Christian celebration, the Christian Pentecost separated from the Jewish Pentecost and moved to the fiftieth day following Easter.

EPIPHANY

A third major festival, Epiphany, became part of the church calendar in the 4th century.[6] This Greek word means manifestation.

> In antiquity an "epiphany" meant either a visible manifestation of a god or the solemn visit of a ruler, who was venerated as a god, to the cities of his realm.[7]

The story of Epiphany is rooted in Egypt where a pagan festival on January 6 commemorated the birth of a sun god. Light, water, and wine (it was believed that on that date springs produced wine) accompanied this festival.

The Egyptian church marked the beginning of the solar year by reading the Gospel of Mark.[8] It begins with the baptism of Jesus. This might explain why Epiphany as an Eastern festival gave equal importance to Jesus' birth,

---

[6] J. G. Davies, ed., *A Dictionary of Liturgy and Worship* (New York: Macmillan Company, 1972), 170.

[7] Adolf Adam, trans. by Matthew J. O'Connell, *The Liturgical Year* (New York: Pueblo Publishing Company, 1981), 144.

[8] Frank Senn, *Christian Liturgy: Catholic and Evangelical*, op. cit., 160-1.

baptism, and first miracle (turning water into wine). All three were manifestations of God in the flesh made visible to humanity.

The Western church adopted this festival but gave it a single focus: the arrival of the Magi with their gifts of gold, frankincense and myrrh.

CHRISTMAS

The origin of Christmas may be related to a dilemma faced by church authorities in Rome. Pagan festivals connected with winter solstice dominated public life. Worship of the sun climaxed on December 25 with gift giving and celebration of light. By establishing a counter celebration at the same time, the faithful might be enticed to abandon the pagan festival and return to the church. Lights in the darkness and gifts for friends and loved ones were easily transferred to worship of Jesus, whose coming was prophesied by Malachi:

> The Sun of Righteousness shall arise
> With healing in His wings;
>
> Malachi 4:2b NKJV

The name is derived from the Roman Catholic Mass for Christ: *Christmas*. The date is fixed. Unlike Easter, which must always be Sunday, Christmas may fall on any day of the week. This fourth major festival of the church year originated in Rome early in the 4th century.[9]

---

[9] J. G. Davies, ed., *A Dictionary of Liturgy and Worship*, op. cit., 135.

MOVEABLE AND FIXED

These four major feast days in the church calendar divide into two kinds: moveable and fixed. The first two feast days, Easter and Pentecost, are calculated by the lunar calendar. They are *moveable feasts* and recalculated every year. They always fall on a Sunday.

The latter two feast days, Epiphany and Christmas, are specific dates on the civic calendar. As such they are *fixed feasts* and occur on the same dates each year. However, from year to year, they occur on different days of the week.

SEASONS OF PREPARATION

As a calendar for the Church took shape, other rituals and ways of observing time emerged. Preparation for major festivals involved many weeks of special prayer and penitence.

LENT

The season of preparation prior to Easter is forty days, symbolic of Jesus' forty days of fasting and testing in the wilderness. It was a time for all the faithful to pray and fast, for sinners to practice extended penance for their wrongdoing, and for converts to prepare for baptism and acceptance into the Church. For many centuries, all baptisms (excepting emergencies) took place on the eve of Easter at a service called the Great Vigil of Easter.

Sundays are always days of celebration and are excluded from these days of fasting and penance. The forty-day period begins on Wednesday. Those first days of Lent, originally for public demonstration of penance by serious sinners, evolved into a corporate service of penance for all the faithful and took the name Ash Wednesday. Whereas earlier penitents had appeared in sackcloth and ashes, contemporary penitents kneel to receive the mark of ashes on their forehead as the beginning of these forty days.

Lent, the name given to these forty days, is from the Anglo-Saxon word for spring: *lencten*.

ADVENT

Christmas is also preceded by weeks of preparation, but generally without the stringent self-discipline expected during Lent. The days of Advent are devoted to penitence and introspection preparing for the celebration of Christ's first coming, and celebrating the expectation of his second coming.

Advent is the English adaptation of the Latin word *Advenus* meaning *coming*.

TWO COMPLEMENTARY CYCLES

The development of major festivals and companion seasons of preparation gradually evolved as the Church added structure into the calendar. Feasting *followed* fasting. Festivity *followed* self-discipline.

The Christmas Cycle is Advent, Christmas and Epiphany.

The Easter Cycle is Lent, Easter and Pentecost.

In both cycles a season of preparation leads to a major festival/season and concludes with a second major festival.

44

Time between the two cycles involves a relatively short period following Epiphany and a lengthy period following Pentecost. Churches vary in how they identify these two in-between times of the church year.

The Roman Catholic church has taken the lead in using the term *Ordinary Time* for both of these in-between-times, as for example: Third Sunday of Ordinary Time.

Some churches prefer an identity that connects in-between-time with the prior festival, as for example: Third Sunday in Epiphany; Third Sunday following Pentecost.

☺ ☺ ☺

ADDITIONAL FESTIVALS

Over the centuries, other major festivals (feast days) have been added to the church calendar. These include Baptism of Our Lord, Transfiguration of Our Lord, Ash Wednesday, Palm Sunday, Maundy Thursday, Good Friday, Ascension of Our Lord, The Holy Trinity, and Christ the King. Each is observed with the appropriate color.

Minor festivals have also been added, such as Reformation Day, All Saints Day, other events in the life of Jesus, celebrations for each of the Apostles and other saints.

AIDS TO KEEPING THE CALENDAR

LECTIONARY

Each time a congregation gathers for worship, scriptures appropriate for the season of the church year are read: one from the Old Testament, one from the New Testament, and one from the Gospels. In addition, the reader or a cantor leads the congregation in responsively reading or chanting a psalm.

These scriptures – pre-selected for every Sunday and festival of the church year – are gathered together in reading units and published in an over-sized book. These scriptures are known as lections. Churches around the world hear these scriptures (and homilies based on them) on the same calendar date.

The book containing the lections is known as the lectionary. It is large and resembles a pulpit Bible. It is kept on the lectern. Use of the lectionary guarantees that scripture will have a significant place in worship each time the congregation gathers. It guards against avoiding difficult texts and dwelling on favorite ones.

The practice of reading scriptures selected for days in the calendar is centuries old. Liturgical churches in all parts of Christendom produced lectionaries appropriate for their needs. The Roman Catholic church, as part of Vatican II reforms, produced and published a three-year set of readings in 1969. Protestant church representatives worked with Catholic bishops to produce an ecumenical version: the *Common Lectionary*. The *Revised Common Lectionary*, published in 1992, is now widely used by Protestant churches.

46

MUSIC

Hymnals in liturgical churches are organized for easy access to hymns for the seasons, festivals and commemorations. In the recently published *Evangelical Lutheran Worship,* the first two hundred hymns are organized for the church year, beginning with Advent and ending with End Time when Christ returns. Each of these pages identifies the season, festival, or commemoration for that hymn in the church year.

Choirmasters and organists select music with the season in mind. Worship planning guides include suggestions for those who need assistance selecting music for the seasons.

COLORS

Colors in the sanctuary change from season to season in churches that observe the church year. The current colors are blue for Advent, white for Christmas through Epiphany, green for Sundays after Epiphany, purple for Lent, white for Easter, red for Pentecost Sunday, white for Trinity Sunday, green for Sundays thereafter through the summer and fall.

Colors change for special times within the seasons. Holy Week, the last week of Lent, may be purple or red until all color is removed for Good Friday. When minor festivals and saints' days are celebrated, red or white is used. Martyrs' days (and Reformation Day in the Lutheran church) are red; celebrations involving Jesus and the saints are white.

The church year is full of activity for those who keep the church dressed appropriately. Each season has a complete set of paraments including hangings for lectern, pulpit, and altar, exquisitely designed and stitched. This treasured fabric art is kept in specially built, long drawers in the sacristy where a color-coded church-year calendar may be found mounted on the wall for consultation. The paraments provide visual opportunities for those who attend worship to feast on the symbols and beauty of the fabric art.

Observance of the church year is rooted in the scripture story of Jesus. His coming (anticipated for centuries), teaching, healing, and miracles; his death, resurrection, and return to heaven; his replacement on earth and promise to come again are included in the story that repeats every year. This story is the basis of the Christian faith.

Through the centuries, the Church has employed oral and visual means to communicate the story. Scripture readings, homilies, hymns, colors, stained glass windows, dramas, paraments, banners, instrumental and choral music have combined to tell the story to people of all ages and cultures, both literate and non-literate.

The scripture story of Jesus – structured by the church calendar – is soul and center for organizing worship in a liturgical church.

CALENDAR CONSTRUCTION

This formula locates the dates necessary for constructing a calendar of the church year. These dates will involve two consecutive years.

EASTER

First, get a civic calendar – one that begins with December of the out-going year. Second, find the date for Easter Sunday and mark the date in the empty blank below.

COUNTING

Count 40 days backwards from Easter, excluding all Sundays, and land on a Wednesday: Ash Wednesday. Mark the date.

Count 50 days forward, beginning with Easter, and land on a Sunday: Pentecost Sunday. Mark the date.

Using December of the out-going year, count 4 Sundays backward from December 25, and land on a Sunday: first day of Advent. Mark the date.

Advent: _____

Christmas: December 25 (a fixed date)

Epiphany: January 6 (a fixed date)

Lent: _____ (Ash Wednesday)

Easter: _____ (Easter Sunday)

Pentecost: _____ (50th day following Easter)

PART III

SPIRITUALITY

Spirituality was not in my vocabulary growing up. My parents valued spiritual things and abhorred worldly things. They never mentioned spirituality.

Moody Bible Institute expected that each student would have a daily quiet time of Bible reading and prayer and thus develop a spiritual life, yet the term *spirituality* was not mentioned.

I have been a member of four Baptist churches. I do not recall hearing the word *spirituality*. If the word was spoken in my United Methodist church, it sailed right over my head.

In the 1980's, *spirituality* as a subject had become popular. Classmates were incorporating it into their degree programs in preparation for future vocations. As a seminary student I acknowledged my need to address this personal gap. A class, titled "Educating Toward Spiritual Development," was offered. The title on the syllabus read: "The Ecology of Spiritual Development." I enrolled.

We were assigned three contrasting approaches to spirituality to study and compare. Then we were to select the model most relevant to our own lives. We read the following:

He That is Spiritual by Lewis Sperry Chafer,
      published in 1918.
Of the Imitation of Christ by Thomas à Kempis,
      1340-1471.
Spirituality and Justice by Donal Dorr,
      published in 1984.

Along with the required written assignments, I drew illustrations of the three models. The Chafer model was an intellectual person with an over-sized head and small heart and hands. This person knows all the scriptures in the New Testament that include the word *spiritual,* and relies on the Spirit to bring proper understanding of them. This is a cognitive approach to spirituality.

The Thomas à Kempis model had a huge heart. This person concentrates on perfecting a personal life that imitates Christ. Meditation and prayer are major commitments. This is a contemplative approach to spirituality.

The Dorr model's heart and head were appropriately sized but arms and legs were oversized. With a passion for social justice, this person joins personal contemplation with public commitment. This is a physical approach to spirituality. I was most

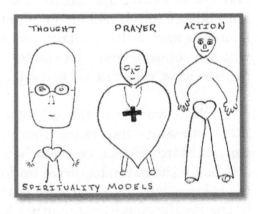

attracted to this model. I like having something to do.

Growing up involved many rules. My parents had multiple expectations or rules (they seemed the same) for how we would function as Christians: things we would do, things we would not do. When I left home and enrolled at Moody Bible Institute, the rules there were similar. Chafer's cognitive model seemed uncomfortably related to multiple rules, emphasizing things that must be done, things that must be avoided.

Thomas à Kempis' contemplative model did not attract me. It seemed to emphasize withdrawal from active involvement in the world. I had not withdrawn. At that time my husband and I lived in Chicago in a Victorian house located two blocks from a major east-west street and one block from a major north-south artery. We were beneath an air corridor for planes circling over Lake Michigan and preparing for descent to O'Hare, one of the busiest airports in the world.

Dorr's physical model seemed most fitting. We lived in the middle of a bustling city. I shared his concern over matters of social injustice. My time at Epworth United Methodist Church included a night spent sleeping with the homeless and multiple nights taking my turn in the gym when my church opened a shelter. I chose Dorr's model as the one most relevant for myself.

Now we live on the side of a mountain in Washington State, one and a half miles from the nearest post office and general store. We see no other house once we exit Highway 9 and begin the extended drive up to our home. Our nearly twelve acres are like a private park. In this new environment in the Pacific Northwest, Native American and Asian religious practices and philosophies abound. I needed to revise and expand my spirituality.

Scripture has been important to me from early childhood, from the stories read to us children every night out of the Bible storybook and from my father's daily readings at the breakfast table. I would not attempt to shape my spirituality apart from scripture. From the cognitive model I chose scripture, not to extract rules for becoming spiritual, but to revel in the stories and the teachings.

Tradition attracted me from the time I walked to church in Lewistown as a little girl in elementary school. From the contemplative model, I chose tradition. It would structure a model of nourishment for me as I changed.

The physical model had directed me to Mother Theresa. I read everything about her that I could find. I admired her balanced spirituality. She did not tire of her commitment to help the poorest of the poor and successfully sustained that passion throughout her entire life. In contrast, I knew people who could *not* sustain their impassioned decision to right wrongs and work for justice, and who then withdrew, choosing another vocation. As she had done, I also would seek to cultivate an intense sustaining inner life. I became increasingly aware of the Holy Spirit and resolved to balance all tasks with prayer – many short prayers.

Nature became part of the mix. My husband and I took on an awesome responsibility when we purchased forested acreage on the side of a mountain. It bore no similarity to the small patch of ground surrounding our house in Chicago, where maintenance included daily removal of trash from our struggling lawn. We had a tree in the back yard that blossomed in the spring. In the front yard we had an overgrown burning bush shrub that had become a tree. The city planted a maple sapling in the narrow strip between sidewalk and curb in front of our house. We watched it grow taller than our house. It felt like our tree. By claiming each of them, we had three trees, more than most people in the city had. Now we have more trees than we can count.

One year before the anticipated move from Chicago to Acme, Washington, the lectionary readings on Trinity Sunday settled my quavering spirit.

Genesis 1:1-2:4a. This lengthy reading of creation gripped my attention. The place we had purchased in northwest Washington State was, without question, beautiful.

II Corinthians 13:11-13 NRSV. "Put things in order . . ." Yes, Lord, I am trying to do that. The attic is almost ready for the move.

Matthew 28:16-20 NRSV. The eleven disciples met Jesus on a mountain. "When they saw him, they worshiped him; but some doubted." I would have done both, feeling very apprehensive and scared. But Jesus did not spend time with the doubts. Instead, "Go . . . And remember, I am with you always . . ."

One tree caught Ray's attention on his first visit to the property. He spotted a cedar tree with three trunks growing as a candelabra and immediately named it the Trinity Tree. Although he had grown up playing and working in the woods, he had never before seen such a tree. It was a sign from God that this was to be our new home. The tree was close to a road. To protect it, he bought discarded railroad ties and built a flower box around it. He filled the box with soil and planted flowers of every color. After learning that the liturgical color for Trinity Sunday is white, I replaced the flowers with white heather. It now fills the entire flower box. In spring the Trinity Tree is surrounded with white.

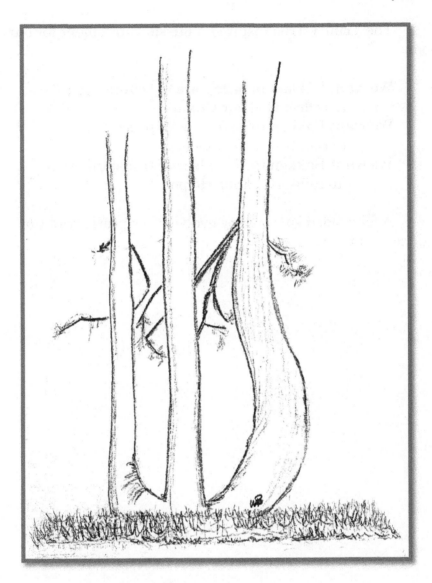

Ray painted a sign.

> *The Trinity Tree:*
> *Father – Creator*
> *Son + Redeemer*
> *Spirit – Helper*

The Trinity Tree inspired a mission statement for our home.

> We want Bakken to be a place of beauty
>> to reflect God our Creator
> We want Bakken to be a place of peace
>> to reflect God our Redeemer
> We want Bakken to be a place of transformation
>> to reflect God our Helper

A four-sided spirituality evolved: scripture, tradition, balance, and nature.

PART IV

PRACTICES

While on a trip to India with my husband, I was invited to visit a woman in her home. The driver delivered me to her front door, then parked and waited. I walked into an elegantly furnished living room. A large coffee table had a single object on it: a beautifully crafted, freestanding brass cross. Many Hindus came to her home. She wanted them to know that hers was a Christian home. When she wondered how to express this, her pastor suggested the cross. Its presence triggered many conversations.

In Bali we discovered that shop owners expected us to avoid stepping into offerings, plates with carefully arranged food and flowers placed in the doorway. Their spirituality as Hindus gave us pause as we arrived.

In Chinese and Thai homes I often noticed small altars where candles were lighted and prayers offered for departed loved ones. Ancestor worship is common throughout Asia. Sometimes I asked questions. Many times I did not. As a guest, I felt privileged to be allowed to see this private place of worship.

One year as I put away the Christmas decorations in my Chicago home, a new thought came to mind. I, too, could involve my home in professing my faith throughout the entire year. None of my friends decorated their homes for Advent, Epiphany, Lent, Easter, or Pentecost. But why not? It would not only be appropriate, but fun.

In the 1980s and early 1990s, as women made their way into ordained ministry in increasing numbers, I completed two seminary degrees. I had no intention of seeking ordination. I was married to a preacher and we did not need two of them in our household. My interest in worship and possibilities for incorporating art in worship prodded me to integrate theology and the arts. But I needed a pulpit. I had things to say. My home became my pulpit.

The church year became a way for me to think through the implications of following Jesus. I wanted to connect faith with life, not just on Sundays when I joined my church family and we worshiped together, but each day of the week.

SCRIPTURE

Selection of scripture is the first step when I design a worship event. Selection of a specific descriptive scripture for each of the seasons was a starting point as I developed practices for my home. But it was not always possible to choose just one scripture reference.

Words in scripture guide *my* choice of words. The choice of translation, when single words are critical, is a significant decision. The multiple translations quoted in this book are individually identified.

WORDS

I wondered whether it would be possible to find a single word to describe each season, one that could be easily remembered. I went a step further. Could each season's story of Jesus' life and the church observance come together in a single word of response, a word that I could personally connect with?

The word project extended over years. While some words came easily, others came with great difficulty and were tossed aside many times in search of better ones. But projects are fun for me. Difficulties only intensified the search. These words may not be my final choice, but these are the ones I now use in shaping my practice of the church year.

Advent – the season of expectation. We wait.

Christmas – the season of joy. God arrives.

Epiphany – the season of discovery. We see.

Lent – the season of testing. We struggle.

Easter – the season of amazement. God Wins!

Pentecost – the season of empowerment. We grow.

HYMNS

After finding a single word to identify each season and my personal response, I searched for compatible hymns and selected these:

Advent: "O Come, O Come, Emmanual"

Christmas: "Once in Royal David's City"

Epiphany: "Here I Am, Lord"

Lent: "How Firm a Foundation"

Easter: "We Know That Christ is Raised"

Pentecost: "The Church's One Foundation"

I am fond of each of these hymns. At the same time, I regret that some have serious limitations as a select set of six hymns for the church year.

In the Advent hymn, the word *Israel* triggers a different meaning today than the 13ᵗʰ century writer had in mind. I wished for another choice that equally claimed my fondness.

Ever since hearing "Once in Royal David's City" sung by a boy soprano at the beginning of Lessons and Carols broadcast from King's College, Cambridge, England, I look for opportunities to include that hymn during the season. It tells the story of Christmas.

For Epiphany, during my experiment using the word *witness* to describe the season, I chose "Here I Am, Lord" by Dan Schutte. But *witness* was not suitable. It had to be explained. Neither word nor hymn was an appropriate choice for this season.

"How Firm a Foundation" always reminds Ray and me of a critical year in our marriage that brought multiple testing. In April of 1965 Ray and I buried our stillborn daughter, weakened by German measles throughout the full-term pregnancy. In July we moved from Seattle to Chicago but found no housing until October. In November Ray was critically burned in a gas explosion and we were homeless again. In February I fell while descending a curved staircase, carrying a basket heaped high with dirty clothes. With my cracked foot in a cast, I hopped on crutches for weeks tending our preschool-aged boys while living on the second floor of a *two-flat*.[10]

For Ray and me, that year was baptism by fire into urban ministry. We had no resources to change our minds and return to Seattle or relocate elsewhere. We had moved to

---

[10] A two-flat is an architectural style in Chicago from the late 1800's. The long narrow brick building has two identical and totally separate living spaces, one above the other, accessed by a common entrance.

Chicago with full confidence that God was leading. Our confidence was never shaken, but was tested to the fullest. That hymn remains a good choice for times of testing. The third verse is our favorite:

> When through fiery trials
> thy pathway shall lie,
> My grace, all sufficient,
> shall be thy supply:
> The flame shall not hurt thee;
> I only design
> Thy dross to consume,
> and thy gold to refine.

Samuel John Stone, 1866

Easter hymns are predominantly from former centuries. Aged. "We Know That Christ is Raised," found in the Lutheran hymnal and written – both text and tune – in the twentieth century, became my choice. But few of my family and friends know it. This hymn can be confusing and difficult to sing.

"The Church's One Foundation" suitably represents the third section of the Apostles' Creed. The drawback, when placed into this collection of choices for distinctive seasons, is recurrence of the word *foundation*. This title is too similar to the Lenten hymn title.

Since selecting these six hymns, I have begun writing hymns. I had no idea that I could. This has been a delightful surprise. They are the result of selecting a distinctive word for each season, plus my personal response to that word.

Most funerals include a favorite hymn of the deceased. My original six choices have now expanded to include fourteen of my own composing. An appropriate hymn for the season can be selected for my funeral when that time comes.

COLORS

In the church, colors are repeated within the church year. White is used for three out of the four major festivals: Christmas, Epiphany, and Easter. Red is used for Pentecost plus Reformation Sunday and for commemoration of martyrs. Green is used for both of the in-between-times following Epiphany and Pentecost, making it the most used of all colors.

After spending years selecting a single word to explain each season, I was not willing to blur the clarity by repeating colors.

During my time as a Methodist, I found permission to deviate from traditional colors in *The United Methodist Book of Worship* on the page "Colors for the Christian Year:"

> Although use of these colors is based
> on broad ecumenical tradition, other
> colors have been and are being used
> in Christian churches. Creativity
> with colors and other signs for days
> and seasons is encouraged.[11]

A practical matter influenced color choices for practicing the church year in my home. In the fifty-one years of our marriage, my husband and I have acquired many things, both as purchases and gifts. We grew weary of this

---

[11] *The United Methodist Book of Worship* (Nashville: The United Methodist Publishing House, 1992), 226.

collection of treasures when they lived with us on a daily basis. The solution was to assign each item to a season. Things out-of-season disappeared into the attic. When the appropriate season arrived, put-aside treasures reappeared. We welcomed them as old friends and enjoyed their company. This plan required a specific time during the year for *all* color possibilities, even those outside my palette of favorites.

A personal conviction entered into the color choices: all colors present in nature are suitable for Christian worship and therefore available to be included in the church year.

Guided by these ideals, I selected distinctive colors for each season of the church year in my home.

ROBES

When our boys were toddlers, my husband bought a small white bust of Johann Sebastian Bach, saying that we

needed to honor this church musician in our home. One day a basketball landed the bust on the floor with head severed from torso. We glued it back together. I fondly refer to this small representation of the master musician as Johann. He has been a part of our family for many years.

One Christmas, before learning about the church year and in a playful mood, I made Johann a red choir robe: a simple lined cape fastened by an antique brass button from my collection. He would have been very busy at this time of year, composing music for his church choirs. When it came time to put away the Christmas decorations, including the new choir robe, he looked unclothed and colorless.

As the plan to profess my faith at home throughout the year evolved, I remembered that Johann Sebastian Bach had composed music for *all* the seasons of the church year. I continued sewing for Johann. He now has a complete set of choir robes, made of fabrics from my scrap drawer. The pattern is kept in the bottom of the robe box, ready for making replacements when more suitable fabric shows up.

Johann denotes the season of the church year at all times by the color of his robe.

BANNERS

The idea of making seasonal banners for my Victorian house in Chicago came to mind in 1988 as I flew home from meeting with artists in Bali. They danced, drummed, recited poetry, displayed photos of paintings and sculpture, and experimented in new forms. As a pianist, I was unable to participate. Bali is not a climate suitable for pianos. The place where we met had no walls! When it rained, we moved ourselves to another location in the room to avoid getting wet. At night, after going to bed, we heard the gamelan orchestras practicing. It was an exotic place. On the flight home I resolved to make banners for each season of the church year. They could be my transportable art to share should I ever have need for that again.

Sewing has been a major part of my life and I have many fabric scraps. My buttons outgrew tins and jars as people learned of my collection and brought me buttons inherited from mothers and grandmothers. I committed to making banners from things I found at home. They would reflect my amateur involvement in the visual arts, my efforts to become a theologian, and my role as a housewife.

This plan remained dormant until the Gulf War of 1991 spurred me to action. The first banner for my home, made during Lent, had three words: "Lord Have Mercy." I hung it on the oak sliding-door casing between the entrance hall and living room of our Victorian house. Everyone coming into our Chicago home would see it.

When Lent ended and the banner came down, the space looked empty. Something had to replace it. My crafting of banners for all seasons began. I wanted each one to explain the season through color, fabric, design, and minimal (if any) wording. Many first efforts were only temporary, replaced by the next time that season came around. Although I was committed to not shopping for supplies, that did not include purchasing fabric found at rummage sales.

ART, ANTIQUES, AND GIFTS

My husband and I enjoy collecting art. Our collection now exceeds the wall space available for display. The extra is kept in the attic waiting its turn. When each new season arrives, I search for appropriate art, either by color or by subject. Not everything is changed, only pieces that must relinquish space to accommodate what we retrieve from storage.

Our collection includes tapestries, lithographs, paintings, watercolors and etchings from around the world. Family and friends have gifted us with art. Having artists

in the family has increased our supply of available items
for the seasons.

Bowls, trays, and pitchers of different sizes, colors, and
materials participate in seasonal changes and are removed
from cupboards and lofty perches to eye-level positions.
Pottery and antique kitchen tools are moved to obvious places
as we renew our acquaintance with gifts received over the
years.

Button-cards, made by a friend who admired my button
collection, are always present, treated as small art pieces.
Miniatures have a special place on the top level of the antique
secretary in our bedroom or on the kitchen mantel.

My vase collection continues to grow by shopping at
rummage sales. One thing I am learning, as I embrace
gardening, is to choose a vase compatible with the flowers
displayed. Just as a one-size garment does not fit everyone,
no single vase suits all flowers equally well.

DISHES

Setting the table with different dishes brings
surprising vitality to the kitchen. If my kitchen were to have
a set of dishes for each of the seasons, including all three
colors chosen for Pentecost, I would happily have a storage
problem. At this point, changing the dishes for each season is
a practice in progress.

We have modest and curious collections of dishes
designated for use at different times. Each season brings new
ways of serving and eating. It is an entertaining adventure.
A cupboard near the kitchen table holds the current set of

dishes. The others are stored in a high cupboard, accessible only by a stepstool.

Two sets of dishes take little to no room in the high cupboard. One set remains in the beginning stage with scarcely enough pieces to accommodate the two of us. The other set is still imagined. For now, dishes for that season are generic white.

Collecting dishes is an enjoyable hobby and fun to pursue as time and opportunity afford. Rummage sales, yard sales, and thrift shops have all  contributed to the supply of dishes in my kitchen. Each set of dishes has different quantities of plates, bowls, and serving pieces. The variety of pieces and the possibility for innovative use make dinner time a light-hearted and enjoyable ending for the day.

☺ ☺ ☺

With a bias to simplify and be practical, and the urge to personalize, I bent a few traditions and developed my own calendar, reclaiming time following Epiphany and Pentecost, and transforming ordinary time into extraordinary time.[12]

_____

[12] Chris Berry coined these phrases about "time" in response to my practice of the church year.

COREAN'S CALENDAR

Advent: season of expectation – we wait
Begins four Sundays before Christmas
Approximately four weeks
Purple, blue, and pink

Christmas: season of joy – God arrives
Begins Christmas Eve
Twelve days
Red

Epiphany: season of discovery – we see
Begins January 6
Includes four to nine Sundays
Orange

Lent: season of testing – we struggle
Begins Ash Wednesday
Forty days
Black

Easter: season of amazement – God Wins!
Begins Easter Sunday
Seven weeks – 49 days
White and gold

Pentecost: season of empowerment – we grow
Begins Pentecost Sunday
Approximately six months divided into thirds
I-spring green II-mature green III-brown

In my home each of the four major feasts initiates a season. Christmas Eve begins the twelve days of Christmas. The Day of Epiphany begins a season that varies in length and may include as few as four Sundays or as many as nine Sundays. Easter Sunday begins a season of forty-nine days, or a week of weeks to celebrate the Resurrection of our Lord. Pentecost Sunday begins the season that stretches over six months. The two preparatory seasons function as usual, with Advent beginning on the fourth Sunday prior to Christmas, and Lent beginning on Ash Wednesday.

Each season ends as the new one begins, leaving no days between without seasonal identity. Every day is placed in a chapter of the unfolding story.

I change to the new season during daylight hours. Decorations to be put away are carried to the attic where an entire wall is lined with boxes marked for each season. Displaced art is stored in the attic. Out-of-season dishes are stored in a high cupboard in the kitchen. I need help making the exchange between what comes out and what returns as I perch on the top of the kitchen stepstool.

Fabrics must be ironed, art selected, and boxes of candles unpacked. The kitchen fireplace mantel is cleared of everything except the antique clock. Vases, stored in a kitchen cupboard, have seasonal assignments, as do soap dishes stored in the supply closet. The cupboard for everyday dishes, the one nearest the table, is emptied, ready to accommodate a fresh set reserved for use during the new season. Banners and large wall hangings are replaced.

Practicing this spirituality in the home was never intended to become another item in the budget, although I keep an eye open for things that will enhance the practice. Even a ten-cent item at my church rummage sale brings freshness and additional meaning. Intentional use of things already at hand is what my practice of the church year is about. But nearly every year something is added. Gifts augment possibilities for the seasons. New ideas and experiments must be tried.

No season has a huge number of decorations. Even so, the amount of time it takes to change the season is substantial. That is why I do not practice observation of single days. They are treated as minor festivals and folded within one of the six seasons.

Seasonal changes are energizing days that bring renewal to the house, and in turn, renewal to our spirits. The change of colors, fabrics, art, and symbols calls attention to each new chapter as the story advances. They are daily reminders to live in the story as I follow Jesus.

PART V

LIFE AT BAKKEN

The season of expectation – we wait

Behold, a virgin shall conceive,

and bear a son,

and shall call his name Immanuel.

Isaiah 7:14 KJV

ADVENT

In my early awareness of Advent, I took a class at Seabury-Western Seminary. Chapel followed immediately after class. I shall never forget walking into an environment transformed by purple. The color eclipsed all else. The richness was spectacularly fitting as we focused on the coming of the Savior.

I continue to give purple first place for Advent, but also include pink and blue.

My Advent banner design was successful on the first try: the silhouette of a pregnant woman in purple wool on a midnight blue background. No lettering was necessary to communicate expectancy.

Johann, in his place of honor on the harmonium (pump organ), dons a purple robe made of the same wool, adorned with an antique brass button. We improvise an Advent banner by pinning a fabric collage of lavender velveteen, lace, ribbons and dried roses onto purple cloth. In the center is a cross.

A small pottery piece with a pregnant Mary riding sidesaddle on a donkey led by Joseph is placed on the fireplace mantel along with candles in blue, purple, and pink. The closing portion of a poem by Tim Bascom, "Waiting for Gabriel," adds a written commentary to the mantel. A bell pull made of Norwegian Hardanger lace hangs from one end, temporarily replacing the bell kept there to announce meals.

In my office a small purple stained-glass piece, in the shape of an arched church window, leans against a large window.

Our dining table and six chairs occupy the center of our great room. On that table I put a purple wool runner with fringe that hangs over the end. A large cobalt blue vase from my mother's funeral is placed on the runner. Our entrance has a comely shoe rack that accommodates footwear when guests arrive. I put a blue wool runner on top, draping the fringe over the ends and adding woven baskets.

In the master bedroom, on the high shelf of the antique secretary, I place small blue gifts given by friends over the years. A tiny tin box from Thailand and a miniature African-American woman made of wood are at eye level as I walk past.

The guest bathroom gets a purple pottery soap dish, made by a friend in the community. It will be joined by purple heather from my alpine garden, placed in a small cobalt blue pitcher purchased from a glass blower in the Ozarks when my sons were small boys.

Two of our son Brian's etchings of scenes in Chicago are hung. One is a solitary woman waiting for the train on a cold deserted elevated platform. The other is the view of a passing train with passengers inside and graffiti below on the train trestle. We hang the deep purple watercolor of a night sky with stars, a gift from one of Brian's students many years ago.

My collection of blue dishes comes down from the high cupboard and moves into the cupboard nearest the kitchen table. A collection it is. Few pieces match. Many shades of blue are involved. It includes two small Mexican bowls decorated with deep blue flowers, and two smaller light-blue porcelain bowls purchased in Hong Kong. At my church rummage sale I purchased a set of six shallow pottery bowls: cobalt blue on the inside and unglazed on the outside. The deep blue glasses were found at a garage sale on a Sunday after leaving church. Ray uses the light blue, deep ceramic bowl for his oatmeal each morning, heaping it to the rim with yogurt and frozen blueberries and raspberries.

On the kitchen table, a single pillar candle rests in the center of a quilted table topper, a gift from the friend who designed and stitched it.

☺ ☺ ☺

Ray prepares for Advent outdoors by hanging blue lights around the entrance of the grotto. This special place deserves its own story.

☺ ☺ ☺

For seven years, after purchasing acreage until our move from Chicago, we spent our summer vacations here at Bakken. The first summer we had only a tent and an outhouse. By the next summer we had a 20 by 14 one-room log cabin made of logs salvaged from a prior owner's beginning attempt to build a log house.

One summer Ray tackled the job of clearing garbage out of a secluded pocket of tall cedars. The trash thrown there included surprisingly large discards: a pink bathtub, several washbasins, and a car door. Ray took two full pick-up loads to the county dump. When all was cleared out, he invited me to come and see the transformed space, saying we now had an outdoor room. What should we do with it?

I pronounced it a grotto and asked him to make benches and a table. We ate many noon meals there on hot days during those vacations. Once we began identifying places at Bakken, it acquired a name: Mary of Nazareth Grotto. Ray hand-painted a sign for it. He then wanted an image of Mary, a Mary who looked Semitic.

Sam Gore, a sculptor and friend of our family, had wanted an excuse to enlarge his small figure of Mary carrying her child. Sam invited Hannah, a young teenager from Lebanon, to model as he reshaped the face with Semitic features. That bronze casting now stands in the grotto. Sam came to supervise the installation. In that secluded place, lighting was needed. Sam wanted a mixture of warm and cool colors: red and blue, one from either side. The historic Church has given significance to those colors: red for theology and blue for humanity. In Orthodox iconography, as Mother of God, Mary wears both colors.

We have hosted Advent meditations in the grotto, bundled in blankets, drinking hot cider.

One year we hosted an Advent party.

Carol, Ray's assistant, asked whether I would host the annual Christmas party for Bakke Graduate University staff. They wanted to drive the ninety miles from Seattle to Bakken and had selected the evening of Sunday, December 3.

I had attended previous staff Christmas parties in homes beautifully decorated for Christmas. On December 3 my house would be decorated for Advent. I asked: Could it be an Advent party? They graciously agreed. None of us had ever been to an Advent party but all were willing to enter into the adventure. I asked that everyone dress in an Advent color: purple, pink, or blue, but not red or green.

Previous parties included gift exchanges. I asked that each person bring a small, gift-wrapped (in Advent colors) box to place on the dinner table as a decoration. The box need not contain a gift, only the hint of a gift to be given at Christmas.

Each person would choose one of the gift-wrapped boxes, open, and try to guess the intended gift.

A lavish number of votive candles, placed on windowsills, welcomed the guests. We began with music: "Sleigh Ride" by Leroy Anderson, arranged for duet and expanded for the occasion to include sleigh bells, Chinese wood block, and cornet. With angklungs (bamboo instruments from Indonesia played by shaking) handed to everyone, we played "Joy to the World" and "Edelweiss."

I sewed matching aprons of dark blue for Carol and me to wear as we became waitresses and served dinner restaurant style. After we cleared away dirty dishes, the decorative gift boxes were opened, one by one. Stories were told around the table, explaining the planning and excitement involved in each gift to be given.

Carol's box contained a single chess piece. She explained about her husband's love of the game. He taught one of their four sons to play chess at age five. That little boy grew up, married and had a son whom he taught to play chess by that same age. The single chess piece symbolized an antique chess set found among her father-in-law's possessions, a surprising discovery since the family has no memory of him playing chess. Carol was excitedly looking forward to wrapping the chess set for her son as a Christmas gift from his grandpa.

Advent activities at Bakken are incomplete without a visit to the grotto. Everyone dressed for outside and walked down the steep path lined with lights. After returning to the warmth of the house, we ate dessert by candlelight and concluded with the reading of a story.

It is the season of expectation. We wait.

JESUS CHRIST, WE SING TO YOU

Jesus Christ, we sing to you,
born to visit earth and die;
Jesus Christ, we give you praise,
risen and returning soon.

Expectations we hold close
in this place of joy and loss.
Guide your Church and keep her safe.
Give her mission in your name.

When disaster rends our world,
filling us with fear and dread,
in the darkness shine your light.
Transform chaos into peace.

As you came in Bethlehem,
come to us in Word and wine.
As you call us to respond,
faithfully we follow you.

Refrain:

God with us, Immanuel.
We your people watch and wait.

From *Aleluya: Singing the Church Year,* by Corean Bakke

85

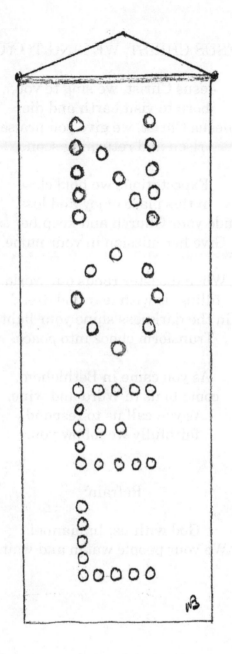

The season of joy – God arrives

And the angel said unto them,

Fear not: for behold I bring you good tidings of great joy,

which shall be to all people.

For unto you is born this day

in the city of David a Saviour,

which is Christ the Lord.

Luke 2:10-11 KJV

CHRISTMAS

Christmas at my church is observed with white paraments. At Bakken, white is used for Easter, the season of highest priority. In keeping with my goal to give each season its own distinctive color and not repeat it, another color had to be chosen for Christmas.

Red combines joy *and* sorrow. In the Luthern church red is the color used when commemorating martyrs, and may be seen as a prophetic color for death. As such it silently conveys the warning spoken by Simeon to Mary in the temple in Jerusalem:

> This child of yours will cause many
> people in Israel to fall and others to
> stand . . . and you, Mary, will suffer
> as though you had been stabbed by
> a dagger.
>
> Luke 2:34-35 CEV

At Bakken we use red for the twelve days of Christmas. We welcome Jesus by holding in tension the festive color for the season and the prophetic color for death, knowing what lay ahead for him and many of his followers.

Preparation for Christmas begins by pinning a hand woven wool blanket from Nagaland, a state in eastern India, onto a rod. Hung in the entrance, it welcomes everyone who comes. Red dominates the striped pattern of brilliant colors. It is the largest of our seasonal hangings.

Two English carolers, made as cloth dolls secured on a base, stand atop the shoe rack with carol books in hand, a gift from years ago.

The Christmas banner is pressed and hung on the post. Made of red felt, the word *Noel* is lettered vertically with large brass shank buttons. An entire jar of matching buttons from my collection was used.

The red velvet robe, lined with red and secured with a brass button, is pressed and put on Johann.

An Ethiopian painting of the Nativity on delicately thin opaque parchment gets special treatment. We remove a batik and replace with this vivid crèche. A Guatemalan triptych crèche is placed on a table next to the kitchen door. A wooden carving of Madonna and Child is hung on the wall.

The fireplace mantel is cleared of everything except the antique clock that strikes the hour. An over-sized round wooden tray, made of ironwood in Zaire, becomes background for a Navaho crèche. My only red dish, a small rectangular tray from Norway, rests against the stones, secured in place with poster putty. A Christmas card with the names for Jesus written in multiple styles of calligraphy stands among tall red tapers. An exquisite paper cut, made by a friend and received as a Christmas card, is stabilized to stand on the mantel.

The dining table in the center of the great room is spread with a white linen cloth bordered with red cross-stitch embroidery. My favorite crèche – Mexican hand-painted pottery figures – is placed in the center. Dinner at this time of year is usually eaten in the kitchen with a fire burning in the fireplace.

A Christmas collection of dishes is not yet begun. All-purpose white dishes must be used. Each evening we light a red pillar candle and eat as it flickers. After dinner I carefully pour off the wax to extend the life of that candle.

In the master bedroom, on the top of the secretary, I put a fringed square of red fabric to stabilize the special cards I display each Christmas: a button snowman card and a button Christmas-tree ornament card, both made by a friend in Chicago who regularly sends button cards.

A red hand-crocheted star-shaped doily given to me in Norway is placed beneath the lamp by the side of the bed.

We do not have an indoor Christmas tree. Ray announced to me, the first Christmas in our new home at Bakken, that he would decorate trees *outside*. Because we would see them through our many windows, they would be our Christmas trees. He draped miniature lights on small trees and bushes. The effect was beautiful.

Not all were clear lights. When he found strings of green, blue, or red, he experimented draping them into recognizable shapes. A treble clef is one of his most persistent shapes. The latest addition to his out-of-doors lighting for Christmas involved outlining the deck with lights. That lighting comes into the house and complements the votive candles we place on the windowsills.

We have a wealth of trees. Cedars and hemlocks tower above us. Once Ray began clearing brush (blackberry vines and other undesirable growth), he planted seedlings. He hopes that eventually they will also grow tall and provide shade to discourage the growth of brush. In the meantime, he is emotionally attached to each of his little trees. None is available for cutting.

But I wished for something inside. I asked whether he could find a dead branch and mount it in the kitchen for indoor lights. He found *two* branches and secured them to the supporting wooden posts in our kitchen. The clear miniature lights immediately won our affection. Those branches have never been taken down. In the long hours of winter darkness, the tiny lights are seen both indoors and outdoors at Bakken.

Twelve days for celebrating Christmas go by too quickly.

It is the season of joy. God arrives.

PLAY YOUR DRUM

Refrain:

Play your drum. Spread the word.
Aleluya, come dance with me.

Verses:

Now at last, Jesus arrives!
Years of long waiting are over.

Born to bring peace to our lives,
Savior for desperate people.

Joy attends news of his birth.
Worship this marvelous coming.

Celebrate! Join in the feast.
Be not afraid! God is with us.

From *Aleluya: Singing the Church Year*, by Corean Bakke

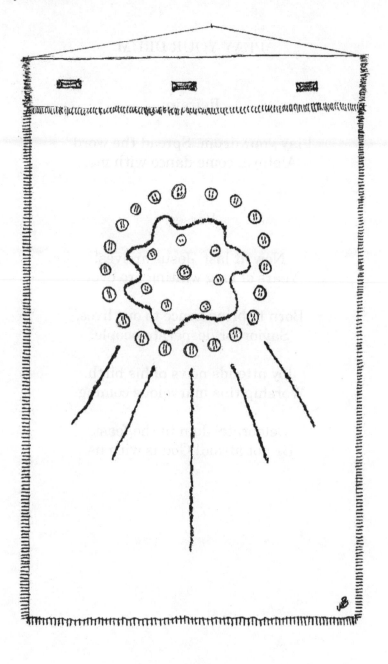

The season of discovery – we see

The people that walked in darkness
have seen a great light:
they that dwell in the land
of the shadow of death,
upon them hath the light shined.

Isaiah 9:2 KJV

Now when Jesus was born in Bethlehem of Judea
in the days of Herod the King,
behold, there came wise men from the east
to Jerusalem saying,
Where is he that is born King of the Jews?
for we have seen his star in the east,
and are come to worship him.

Matthew 2:1-2 KJV

Jesus spoke to them, saying,
"I am the light of the world.
Whoever follows me will never walk in darkness
but will have the light of life."

John 8:12 NRSV

EPIPHANY

A color for Epiphany at Bakken required a new choice.
At Our Saviour's Lutheran, white is used for Epiphany
Sunday and green for Sundays following. At Bakken, white is
reserved for Easter and green for Pentecost. Neither color
could be repeated for Epiphany. Whatever the choice, it
should be meaningful, one that could symbolize light in the
darkness.

Orange! I thought of paintings with great balls of fiery
light in the sky. Orange! Worn by repairmen working in
dangerous places, painted on traffic cones and emergency
signs, it attracts attention. Orange! It has never been a color
I enjoy, perhaps because I cannot wear it. However, with its
position on the color wheel (secondary color) it is important.
If I genuinely open myself to using all color possibilities in
my home, there must be a place for orange.

One evening dinner guests arrived at Bakken with a
plant I had never seen before: Crocosmia. It had delicate deep
orange blossoms. I planted it in my main flower garden,
hoping to develop appreciation for it. But each time I walked
past, the color annoyed me. It did not blend with the other
flowers.

With a number of gardening problems to solve, I
invited Vanessa to come for a visit. I call her my gardening
consultant when I need help making outdoor decisions. I call
her my personal shopping consultant when I need something
that she is likely to discover.

Aware of my admiration for the Dutch artist known for
sunflowers, she suggested that I have a Vincent van Gogh

Garden. All attention-getters could be together in that garden. The ability of orange to grab attention is the very reason I chose it for Epiphany.

As this past Epiphany season approached, I searched the house for something to hang in the entrance and found a piece of forgotten fabric art in the library. We improvised a banner by pinning the Balinese batik onto a tablecloth. The artist's design shows Jesus opening the eyes of a blind man, both of them contextualized as Balinese. The colors are perfect; the subject is perfect. Why had I never thought of it before?

The banner was made years ago. For the darkness of Epiphany, I used a dark brown wool tweed cloth. For the great light I gathered orange buttons and wished for beads to make rays. With none on hand and certain that they were essential for the design, I broke my rule in making this banner by visiting a bead shop. Several Epiphanies came and went before all the beadwork was completed. The laborious effort to hand-stitch hundreds of tiny beads resulted in a design visible from only inches away. Someday, when I have accumulated enough small orange buttons, I hope to correct this mistake.

Johann's polyester robe is much too common looking for this season. I look forward to replacing it with a robe made of rich tapestry, the kind of cloth I might someday find in a rummage sale.

I place an elegant Persian cloth on the dining table, a gift from Ray's Iranian student, and center a tall, bright-orange glass vase on top. It catches sunlight, reflecting an orange tint onto our white walls. A soft peach-colored shawl

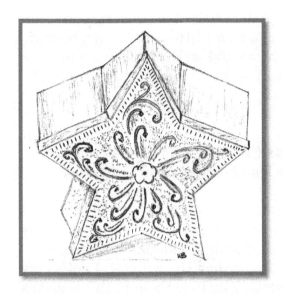

drapes a table next to the kitchen door. A white, star-shaped box is the solitary ornament. This table is a tempting temporary landing place for items on their way to other parts of the house. The star will successfully redirect clutter.

The antique pump organ, where Johann resides, has a rounded candleholder on either side. I put orange-tinted pillar candles there, purchased after much searching.

I clear the fireplace mantel of everything except the antique clock that strikes the hour. From the storage box I remove a worn wooden shoe that reminds me of my paternal German Dutch ancestry. I place it on the mantel facing the scripture verse from Isaiah: "The people that walked in darkness have seen a great light . . ."

The framed picture from a calendar reminds me of the time I was church-homeless and concerned, wondering when and where I might find a new church home. I was invited to an Epiphany party where everyone was asked to select a picture and

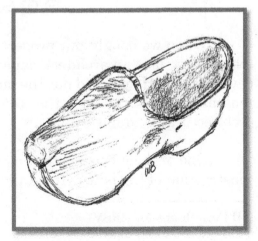

explain its significance. The darkness of an underground cave with a small spot of light caught my attention. It symbolized my anxiousness. I took it home and on the backside wrote: "For we walk by faith, not by sight."[13] It rests on the mantel secured by poster putty.

We hang an etching carried home from Bombay. Titled "Flight to Egypt," it depicts the heads and faces of the Holy Family profiled by Mary's long hair swept straight back in their haste.

An orange hand-painted tray is placed on the secretary in the bedroom. In my office, a small landscape watercolor with a splash of orange leans against the window. I polish my copper pieces and conspicuously include them in this season's decorations.

Mealtime keeps us humble. The cupboard next to the kitchen table is mostly empty. We have four plates, two bowls, and two mugs for the season. A unique orange pillar candle lightens the darkened kitchen each evening. From the first-time lighting of the wick, the entire candle glowed from top to bottom.

☺ ☻ ☺

When we bought our property, Ray's friend from high school days, now an architect, came to counsel us about site development. He pointed out the many snags – standing remnants of trees – saying that they must be left in place as architectural landmarks.

One of them became the eastern point on line for construction of the house. It is tall and has a curious bulb

---

[13] II Corinthians 5:7 NRSV

growth on top. We see it prominently from our large windows. The growth on top reminds Ray of the domes on Eastern Orthodox churches and symbolizes for him the tenacity of a church that has endured centuries of hardship and persecution. Ray named it the *Epiphany Tree*. He recently transformed the basement into a classroom with windows that frame that ancient snag.

It is the season of discovery. We see.

DISCOVERY PENETRATES DARKNESS

Refrain:

Discovery penetrates darkness
as light shines on the path.
Epiphany miracles still appear,
transforming us for life.

Verses:

Wisemen follow the star,
looking for a child.
They worshiped him with gifts
of frankincense, myrrh, and gold.

Jesus asked for a drink,
causing great surprise!
He promised living water,
life without thirst again.

On a mission to find
Christians and arrest,
a light and voice stopped Saul,
reversed and renamed him Paul.

Peter, taking a nap,
three times saw a dream;
God teaching him respect
and care for all living things.

Luther, reading the Book,
found the truth at last.
The just shall live by faith
alone without works or fear.

Questions endlessly rise
prodding us to search,
yet we believe God's word
that all those who seek shall find.

From *Aleluya: Singing the Church Year*, by Corean Bakke

The season of testing – we struggle

Then Jesus was led up by the Spirit

into the wilderness

to be tempted by the devil.

Matthew 4:1 NKJV

Trouble produces endurance,

endurance produces character,

character produces hope.

Romans 5:3-4 Moffatt

LENT

Nine chairs that I refinished now have black leather seats. The antique fainting couch in my office is upholstered in black. The metal fittings for the exposed beams in our house are black. My seven foot Mason-Hamlin piano is black. My pottery includes black bowls and jugs from Japan, South Africa, Congo, and New Mexico.

With a wealth of black treasures, I wanted a time for that color. Lent was my choice of season for black, the color suggested by the ashes of Ash Wednesday and the color sometimes used for Good Friday. In our rainy climate we use black sparingly.

The hanging on the high rod in the entrance is a Chinese tapestry of the Last Supper, nearly unrecognizable in its originality.

The banner for the post is black. After rejecting the first and second Lenten banners, I succeeded on the third attempt. The process of *unweaving,* where threads are removed to create a design, resulted in a beautiful black banner. The missing threads outlined the shape of a cross, exposed when mounted on the post. No words were necessary.

Johann's robe is black velvet. This fabric is not liturgically appropriate for Lent. Sackcloth, the biblical fabric connected with repentance, would be ideal, but my only piece of sackcloth is a small table-topper sent by a friend living in the Middle East. I always make a place for it during Lent and encourage guests to touch it. Sackcloth is woven of goats' hair:

dark in color, thick, coarse, and unpleasantly rough and itchy. I cannot imagine wearing it in the hot temperatures of the Middle East.

My rational for a velvet robe relates to the way Ray and I have responded to times of testing in our marriage. When circumstances were grim, we made a party of whatever we had on hand. Black velvet is Johann's performing robe *and* party robe for Lent.

From black velvet, I cut random shapes and pieced them together with crazy-quilt hand stitching, then faced with lining fabric. This small decorative square is placed beneath the lamp next to our bed. A companion piece is the patched Bedouin cooking pot purchased in Amman, Jordan, and scrubbed for years. The patchwork of intersecting metals is now clearly visible. Both patched items – the cooking pot and the velvet piece – remind me of broken lives mended and restored to beauty and service. God transforms bad into good.

On top of the shoe rack I place a black runner with fringe. Made in China, it has subtle patterns in deep red woven into velvety fabric. I select button cards from *Who Has the Button?*[14] to place on top. Each card interprets a scripture verse from the lectionary for Sundays in Lent. Some are simple. Many are complex. A few are disturbing. All are thought provoking. The set includes more cards than I can display at one time.

I clear the fireplace mantel of everything except the antique clock that strikes the hour and place black tapers in pewter candleholders of different sizes. A lithograph is placed among the tapers. Black on white, designed and printed by our youngest son, it shows a homeless woman of his acquaintance washing her feet as she leans against a building for support. He sent it one year as a Mother's Day gift and wrote a letter on the back. I ought to frame it. How can I frame it without hiding the letter? Which is more precious?

A tile of two women wearing black clothing that completely covers all but their eyes is on the mantel. I put it there eight years ago, when, at the end of the mid-week Lenten service on 19 March 2003, the pastor announced that US planes were bombing Iraq. That tile has remained on the fireplace mantel ever since, reminding me to pray for the women of Iraq as I work in my kitchen. I vowed to leave it there through every season until that war came to an end. When I write about clearing the mantel in preparation for the new season, keep in mind that a small tile never leaves.

---

[14] *Who Has the Button?* by Marcia Whitney-Schenck. February-April 2003 Lenten meditations inspired by Corean Bakke's button collection.

☺ ☺ ☺

We have many crosses and four other interpretations of the Last Supper. Two of them remind us of Da Vinci's famous painting: a metal *repoussé/chasing* and an African painting. The Russian painting and a pottery piece from St. Andrews Abbey in Valyermo, California, are totally different.

Our collection of black pottery appears. The most recent addition, a Tarahumaran[15] cooking pot, a gift for our fiftieth wedding anniversary, is placed on a low shelf, framed against the white wall.

My Lenten dishes recall a story from the first year of my marriage. I became friends with a woman who lived in a house painted black. Sensing that I was lonely, she often invited me to her home. We had lunch together many times: simple food served on black dishes. I learned how beautifully food displays on black dishes. That was the beginning of my appreciation for black.

Sometime later my mother happened to be with a friend who had a set of black Melmac dinnerware to give away. I became the recipient. Those plates are the nucleus of my dishes for Lent. Supplements to the original set include a set of black-tinted water glasses. I made black napkins. Table settings during Lent are dramatic.

☺ ☺ ☺

The water system at Bakken has been an ongoing struggle from the beginning. It has tested Ray's patience beyond anything else.

---

[15] The Tarahumara people, Native Americans, live in northern Mexico.

When we purchased land in the Pacific Northwest, known for rain forests and constant precipitation, we had no idea we would have problems getting a reliable source of water. The village of Acme, a mile and a half to the north, had an excellent well. We had to drill our own well. A dowser came and witched a site for the well. It was drilled down to 325 feet precisely on that site.

But one day in July while here on vacation, before moving from Chicago, we learned the limitations of our well. The water supply ran out in the middle of Ray's shower.

In order to get a building permit we had to prove the presence of a plentiful and safe supply of water. Ray had a sample taken in the rainy season, hoping to qualify for the permit. The permit was issued.

Drought set in and summer after summer got drier. We went from the well to the creek, hoping to solve our problem. Rusted iron water pipes, found on our property near the creek, attest to former water problems. For two successive summers, the creek dried up on the same day, July 25. We purchased a green water tank for the back of the truck and began carrying water. Bathrooms were equipped with buckets of water for flushing. People who came to visit, knowing of our predicament, brought jugs of water as gifts.

The water table dropped. Our well was drilled deeper to a depth of 520 feet. Ray installed outdoor tanks that could be filled with water during rainy times and supplement our well in dry times. A neighbor designed and helped him install a system of underground pipes to route water for filling and emptying tanks.

This is only part of the story but you get the idea. So far, there has been no end of the things that can go wrong and have to be solved.

Testing is always a time of struggle. It does not necessarily come during Lent, but Lent lends resources for coping, whenever that time arrives.

It is the season of testing. We struggle.

DOES ANYBODY CARE

I'm beaten, afraid, lonely,
lonely.
Every day is a great struggle,
O Lord.

When will these tears end, pain and
tears end?
What about each of my children?
O Lord.

My questions all night haunt me,
haunt me.
Is it wrong that I feel hatred?
O Lord.

God tell me. I must listen,
listen.
Is there hope? Can you solve problems?
O Lord.

Refrain:

Does anybody care?
Does anybody care?
Does anybody care?
Lord have mercy.

From *Aleluya: Singing the Church Year*, by Corean Bakke

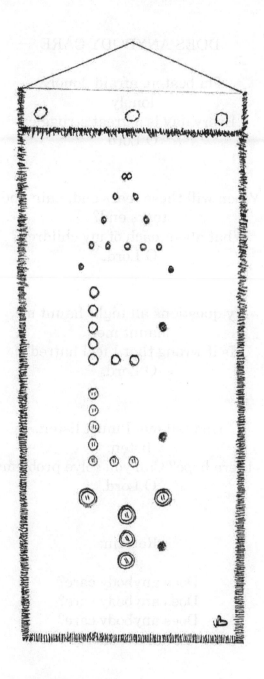

The season of amazement – God Wins!

Do not be alarmed;

you are looking for Jesus of Nazareth,

who was crucified.

He has been raised;

he is not here.

Look,

there is the place they laid him.

But go, tell his disciples . . .

So they went out and fled from the tomb,

for terror and amazement

had seized them;

and they said nothing to anyone,

for they were afraid.

Mark 16:6-8 NRSV

EASTER

White and gold for Easter reconcile colors at Bakken with the church color calendar. Moving from Lent to Easter is the most dramatic of all seasonal changes in our home. It intensifies the drama between death and resurrection. I move about the house, removing everything black that appears only during Lent.

A white banner with brass buttons replaces the black banner hanging on the post. This banner was successful on the first try. On an off-white strip of fabric, left over from making shades for my Victorian house in Chicago, I stitched an assortment of brass shank buttons in a vertical design, spelling the word *aleluya* with the beginning vowel only and the following consonants: A L L Y. The left-out vowels are indicated with small brass buttons off to the right. Hebrew spelling works this way. It omits vowels.

Johann discards the black robe and changes into a white satin robe made with scraps from a daughter-in-law's wedding dress. This is his most elegant robe, but the most unbecoming to his white complexion.

An antique white linen runner replaces the black-fringed runner on top of the shoe rack. Hand-painted parchments from Ethiopia replace the Lenten button cards. Each parchment depicts wide-eyed, white-robed, dark-skinned people busy in an activity, many of them playing traditional musical instruments.

We hang an etching of three women excitedly walking away from the empty tomb. The artist, Joan Bohlig, lettered Matthew 28:5-7 around the print as a border.

The black Melmac dishes return to the high cupboard and white dishes move into the cupboard nearest the kitchen table. This is the season when I gather and polish the brass pieces. A large brass bowl becomes the centerpiece on the dining table.

After clearing the kitchen fireplace mantel of everything except the antique clock that strikes the hour, I fill my two unmatched brass candlesticks with white tapers and place them on the mantel along with an antique hammered brass tray. White pillar candles of various sizes join the tapers. The framed copy of an ancient mosaic – Jesus blessing the catch of fish – is given a place among the candles.

A small brass vase, a gift brought by a guest from India, is filled with white heather from the alpine garden and placed in the guest bathroom.

Daffodils and budding forsythia branches inspire bouquets of all sizes.

I remove our sizeable collection of crosses and make room for *Easter Triptych,* the centerpiece of our Easter decorations. Two boxes must be carried down the ladder from the attic. My sewing table in the workroom is moved into the great room and placed directly beneath a large window. I unpack the art piece made by Martha Emmert, carefully unwrapping each delicate piece. Martha taught art as her mission assignment in Zaire. With no budget for supplies she rescued things thrown away, transforming trash into treasures. She proudly wore the title: junk artist.

118

A tomb constructed of clay is placed in the center of the table, toward the back. A flat clay stone, made to cover the tomb entrance, can be easily moved. Inside is a low bench and white linen napkin. I reconstruct a garden of items Martha

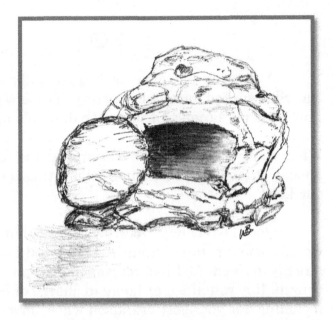

assembled, molded from clay, or gathered from her travels: a pool made of a mirror bordered with small polished stones and tiny clay water jug; palm trees, flower gardens, and whimsical plants made of dried coffee roots. By locating the tabletop scene in front of a window, outdoor trees become an extension of this indoor garden.

Easter Triptych includes all three events from the story of Jesus' burial in a garden tomb. Two Roman soldiers with shiny shields and long spears occupy the left side. They have a round table for their dice, quill pen and ledger, and a picnic table and benches for passing the time as they guard the tomb. Three women carrying spices approach the tomb, walking a path lined with stones, and encounter an angel. On the right, Mary Magdalene bows before the risen Christ.

I wonder why it took me so long to imagine a tabletop display of the resurrection and to commission an artist to make it. A junk artist was the perfect person to create this Easter art piece.

119

☺ ☻ ☺

A sister-in-law gave me bags of bulbs a few years ago. She worked for a bulb nursery. These were overstock. I outlined my largest garden with daffodils and planted daffodils randomly up and down the North Bank Garden. When those flowers open in the spring and forsythia blossoms appear, it feels like Bakken is celebrating the Resurrection of our Lord.

One Easter, Ray received the call that his mother would come for the morning. Our son and his family had already arrived. As I had responsibilities at my Lutheran church, Ray remained at home in charge of hosting everyone, including our youngest grandson whose favorite thing at Bakken was the John Deere tractor. He often sat on Ray's lap for rides and was learning to steer.

Ray's mother was in a wheel chair. Rather than take her to the little church in Acme, Ray planned a homily at home, outside in the alpine garden, telling the story of Jesus' death and resurrection. Afterwards, hoping to make both events understandable for Elijah, about to turn four years old, the two of them went to the nearby Saxon Cemetery. There the Easter story continued in the presence of family gravesites. When Ray finished, he asked Elijah whether he had any questions.

"When the tractor dies and we bury it,
will it rise again? Like new?"

It is the season of amazement. God Wins!

ALELUYA

Refrain:

Aleluya, aleluya.
Aleluya, aleluya.
Aleluya, aleluya.
Aleluya.

Verses:

God became man in Bethlehem,
Jesus his name, his mission plain:
preaching and teaching and healing the sick.

Witnessed by all, followed by some,
God in the flesh made a big stir.
Enemies plotted to put him to death.

After three days Jesus arose!
Evil could not maintain control.
With great amazement the truth became known.

Life conquered death. Hope hushed despair.
Joy displaced fear as friends believed.
Jesus became proof that God always wins!

From *Aleluya: Singing the Church Year*, by Corean Bakke

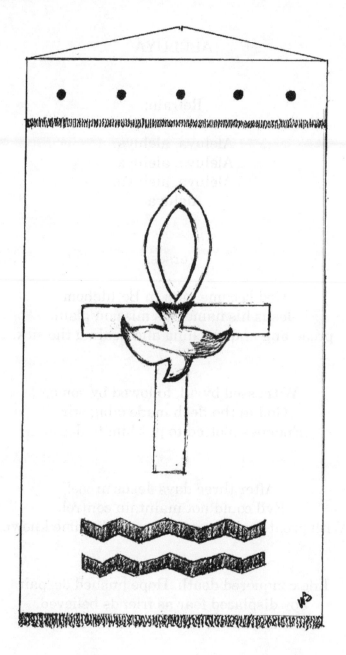

The season of empowerment – we grow

All of them were filled with the Holy Spirit

and began to speak in other languages

as the Spirit gave them ability.

Acts 2:4 NRSV

For God has not given us a spirit of fear,

but of power

and of love

and of a sound mind.

II Timothy 1:7 NKJV

PENTECOST

This is the season I divide into three parts to avoid six months of the same color. I liken spiritual growth to the growth surrounding me out of doors and chose relevant colors: spring green for early growth; hunter green for the period of maturity; brown for dormancy, the end of the growing season. Each of these divisions has its own banner. I distinguish between the three divisions by identifying them as I, II, and III.

PENTECOST I

Pentecost I banner has a light green background. Red, always used in the church for Pentecost, is present as a descending dove. Shading on the dove (p. 122) indicates royal blue. These vivid colors were cut from African batik. This first banner of the lengthy season is a visual interpretation of the third part of the Apostles' Creed:

"I believe in the Holy Spirit" – a descending dove cut from red and royal blue African batik

"the Holy Catholic Church" – a white wedding-satin cross

"the communion of saints" – four small blue fabric-covered buttons at the top, holding the fold-over in place

"the forgiveness of sin" – a wavy strip cut from
that same red and blue African batik

"the resurrection of the body" – another wavy
strip

"and the life everlasting." – a loop of white satin
on top of the cross, converting it to an ankh, the
Egyptian symbol for everlasting life.

The banner is pressed and hung on the post. I can see it
from the kitchen island as I prepare meals. As a Lutheran-in-
progress, I still must concentrate when reciting the creed.

Johann's white satin Easter robe is replaced with a
jaunty robe of spring green fastened with a round green glass
button. From his perch on the organ, he looks down at the two
spring green pillar candles positioned on the organ's
candleholders. They were difficult to find. I shall burn them
sparingly.

On the high rod in the entrance Ray hangs a Chinese
tapestry of Jesus as the good shepherd. The pasture is both
spring green and mature green. We will use it until October.
A spring green runner is placed on top the shoe rack.

Since seeing oriental rugs used on tables in
Amsterdam, I have adopted this custom and use a small
celery-green rug on the dining table for Pentecost I as a
reminder of my German Dutch heritage. Long stemmed white
daises are in bloom. I make an extravagant bouquet.

From Ray's library I borrow his specially commissioned
icon of reconciliation: Paul and Barnabas, with John Mark
between them. Those remarkable men eventually patched up

their strained relationship over an undocumented episode that occurred on Paul's first missionary journey.

From the taper candle storage I remove boxes marked Easter and Pentecost I. The white candles of Easter are wrapped in paper to protect them from discoloring or bending during the summer and packed into the Easter box. Spring green tapers in various lengths are found in the Pentecost I box. I use candles all the way to the bottom. Differing heights add interest. White pillar candles are not boxed, but shelved, including the tall one used as a Christ candle.

The fireplace mantel is cleared of everything except the antique clock that strikes the hour. The ironwood tray from Zaire returns from the attic. Its enormous size covers many of the fireplace chimney stones and makes an ideal background for delicately colored and detailed objects. From an upper cupboard I bring down a porcelain fisherman holding his bamboo pole, a gift from China. It reminds me of Jesus' parting words: "Go . . . and make disciples of all nations . . ."[16]

To the left of the fireplace, in a niche for the highchair, there is space for hanging small pictures. I hang a painting of women in Bali, working in the rice fields. A volcanic mountain is seen in the background. Pentecost is when I enjoy gathering reminders of people and places around the world.

In the bedroom, on the top shelf of the secretary, I place a traveling-size triptych of Mary, Mother of our Lord. The coloring is perfect for these first two months of Pentecost. She greets me each morning as I walk past.

---

[16] Matthew 28:19 NRSV

Ray surprised me one year on the Saturday before Pentecost Sunday with a box of dishes purchased at a garage sale: eleven dinner plates plus dessert plates, bowls and cups in descending numbers. They more than fill the cupboard nearest the kitchen table. White with a narrow green band around the edge, they have become our dinnerware for the beginning months of Pentecost Season: June and July.

In my office I place a round, mostly-green piece of art glass on the windowsill.

PENTECOST II

The season of empowerment – we grow

PENTECOST II

The second section of this long season begins in August, when rain ceases. The climate of the Pacific Northwest changes from dampness to drought. The rug comes off the dining table. With windows open, it is more practical to have no fabric when dusting is a more frequent chore. Bouquets from now to the end of the season will be placed on the bare table. A slender stone vase of dark green, purchased at a garage sale, is perfect for hydrangea blossoms with all the greenery removed.

An Ethiopian hanging, with three different Coptic crosses stitched in hunter green, is hung on the post. Johann puts on his hunter green velveteen robe. A hunter green runner replaces the spring green runner on the shoe rack.

From the fireplace mantel, the Chinese fisherman returns to a high cupboard reserved for breakables. A very small Chinese teapot, partially glazed with dark green, is carefully placed on the mantel. Each time I remove it from the high cupboard, I move slowly, hoping to not bump anything. It is not a functional teapot, but a fragile work of art. I remove the spring green candles, both pillars and tapers, and replace them with dark green.

I hang a pair of brightly colored hand-knitted wool socks from the fireplace mantel. They arrived at my home all the way from Kazakhstan where a young woman grew up in a Muslim home. Through astonishing happenings she converted to Christianity and escaped the "honor killing" usually awarded to such family members. Following completion of secondary school, she came to this country to continue her education and met my sister's daughter who brought her home on a vacation break. The socks were a hostess gift. They remind me – when I forget – that the Holy Spirit is at work in our world choreographing events and transforming lives.

A recent gift is now framed and has become part of Pentecost II: an ancient Irish blessing lettered in elegant calligraphy.

> May the road rise to meet you,
> May the wind be always at your back,
> May the sun shine warm upon your face,
> May the rains fall soft upon your fields,
> And, until we meet again,
> May God hold you in the hollow of His hand.

We hang it near the front door. Summer months are traveling time.

Batiks of women maintain their place on the walls: a procession of Kenyan women carrying loads of water, food, and firewood; an African mother and child with ornate detailing in their hair and jewelry. International art is especially appropriate for this season of Pentecost when the Church spread beyond Jerusalem into other countries.

The large set of dishes returns to the high cupboard. I remove a smaller set of white dishes with wide, dark green borders. Miscellaneous additions, purchased at garage sales and my church rummage sale, slowly augment this set of dishes.

PENTECOST III

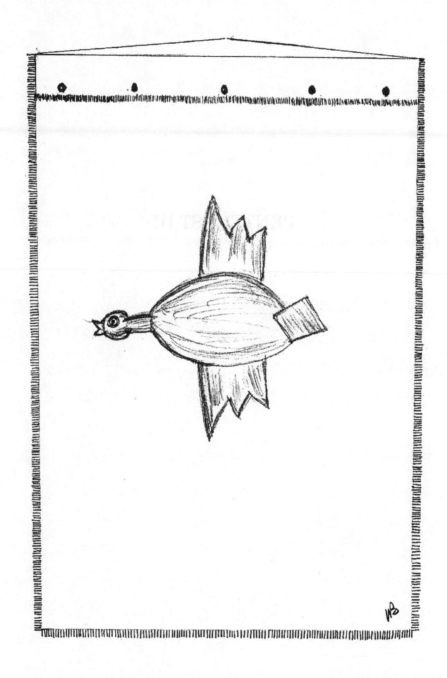

The season of empowerment – we grow

PENTECOST III

The final third of the long season begins with October and continues through November until Advent begins. This is the final color change in my home: from mature green to brown for the remainder of the church year.

My banner displays an ancient Celtic symbol of the Holy Spirit, a wild goose in flight that can neither be predicted nor controlled. I replicated this symbol in fabric using browns, hunter green, mahogany, and white and stitched it on a light brown remnant of coarse linen.[17]

Johann dons a warm rust-brown corduroy robe, the remaining one in his wardrobe box yet to be worn. The shoe rack is covered with a richly patterned brown runner that hangs over the ends with fringe. Hand woven baskets are placed on top of the fabric.

From Ray's library I borrow a watercolor: two jeepneys crowded with people inside and recklessly loaded on top with boxes and goats. The artist positioned one jeepney approaching, the other departing. Slogans – "God's Ways Are Many" and "Never Despair" – are painted above the front and rear windshields. Usually hidden among books in Ray's library, this depiction of life in Ghana comes to the entrance hall to be enjoyed up close.

I cut an armload of Autumn Joy sedum and arrange an enormous bouquet for the dining table. An antique milking-machine bucket, now rusted brown, serves as a dramatic over-

---

[17] This sketch is based on the logo of the Wild Goose Resource Group of the Iona Community, copyright @ WGRG, Iona Community, Glasgow G2 3DH, Scotland. www.wgrg.co.uk

sized vase. These flowers gradually dry as the water supply depletes. They last until Advent.

On an antique set of open shelves, I place wooden bowls collected from near and far. A hand-made pottery vase, a gift to complement the earth tones of my kitchen, is filled with white hydrangea blossoms.

The fireplace mantel is cleared of green and arrayed with brown on either side of the antique clock that strikes the hour. A pair of onyx candleholders from Mexico holds caramel-colored candles. Antique wooden kitchen tools from Norway and Holland are stabilized with poster putty.

Fabric art is pressed: Ozark acorns painted on a beige background; a hand-made Ethiopian tablecloth with Coptic crosses in fall colors.

The final set of dishes is removed from the high cupboard: sand colored pottery with a narrow brown border. On special occasions we replace these dishes with wooden goblets, bowls and plates made of mahogany in Haiti.

☺ ☺ ☺

This longest season of the church year has given me extended time to grow. When Ray and I moved to the Pacific Northwest, I knew nothing about gardening, nor was I interested in learning. Almost immediately I realized that would have to change. In this rainy temperate climate, everything grows profusely without encouragement. Abandoned or neglected houses can disappear behind natural vegetation. Blackberry vines grow aggressively. Their strong and sharply barbed canes grow tall, arching overhead if undeterred.

When Ray's cousin brought us abandoned plants from the greenhouse nursery where he worked, they nearly died waiting for me to plant them. No time of day seemed the right time to go outside and get dirty. I had cancer-prone skin. Sunlight was dangerous for me. Excuse followed excuse.

I am a morning person. Challenges are best handled at the beginning of the day. I would have to garden first thing! And so I did, changing out of my nightgown into bib overalls. Without a single bite of breakfast, nor a cup of coffee (which I never drink anyway), I put on a wide-brimmed straw hat and marched myself out the door.

I weeded, planted, watered, and established boundaries for the spaces I would tend. Diva and Maestro, my outdoor cats, accompanied me. Together we listened to the sounds of early morning and breathed the fragrant air. I learned to enjoy crawling in the dirt before the heat of the day. It became my special time with God, allowing myself to be transformed.

Our acreage, on the side of a mountain, is divided between an upper part and a lower part with our house in the middle. The upper part ascends following a creek and canyon on the north. The western boundary crosses the width of our plot while continuing to climb. The southern boundary descends steeply to the driveway and our house. When Ray discovered this pattern of up – across – and down he staked a trail of two thousand feet following these boundaries.

While still in Chicago, before our move, he spent an entire winter thinking through the centuries of church history. He chose a significant person from each of the twenty centuries since Christ. He honored the group by calling them his *mission saints*. Each of them crossed boundaries and carried the story of good news beyond the orbit of established Christendom.

138

On each vacation trip to Bakken, this trail took shape as Ray looked for the best path through the forest. He built stairs where the grade was too steep to walk safely. He built a bridge where a large rock defied removal. He installed drainage pipes to channel water that persistently washed the trail away. He carried gravel to fill muddy holes. In the end, he made twenty markers, installed them one hundred feet apart, and hammered a number on each.

These saints represent Eastern and Western churches. Ray takes great pleasure in sharing the stories of how they lived their faith with boldness and purpose. He has conducted countless tours of his trail and written a book about it. [18] The trail has become a walking exhibit of global mission.

It is the season of empowerment. We grow.

---

[18] Ray Bakke, *A Surprising Journey: From Saxon to Chicago and Back* (Acme, WA: Bakken Books, 2009).

HOLY SPIRIT, COME TO THIS PLACE

Holy Spirit, come to this place.
Settle our fears, remind us how to pray.
Scatter doubts and open our eyes
to tasks that you would have us do.

Holy Spirit, live in our hearts.
Help us to make decisions in your name.
Teach us daily ways to remain
faithful and fruitful to the end.

Holy Spirit, fill us anew.
Give us the grace to act and speak your love.
Make us salt and light for the world.
Shape us and grow us as you will.

From *Aleluya: Singing the Church Year*, by Corean Bakke

The last Sunday of Pentecost Season is Christ the King Sunday. It brings the church year to conclusion by focusing on the day in the future when Jesus will return. The eucharistic liturgy throughout the year includes the response: "Christ has died. Christ is risen. Christ will come again."

The question through the centuries has been, *When?*

I ask myself that question as the antique clock on the mantel strikes the hour.

> Watch therefore, for you do not know
> what hour your Lord is coming.
>> Matthew 24:42 NKJV

WHEN WILL JESUS COME

When will Jesus come
and renew the world?
Days and months and years go by
and yet he does not come.
You forget the words he said:
I am coming very soon.
I am coming very soon.

When will justice win
over lies and greed;
no one hungry, no one homeless,
no one destitute?
You forget the words he said:
You are light for all the world.
You are light for all the world.

When will evil end
and the violence cease?
Fear increases. Threats grow stronger.
Where shall we go hide?
You forget the words he said:
Do not be afraid. Believe!
Do not be afraid. Believe!

When will crying cease
and emotions heal:
no more sickness; no more dying;
no more broken hearts?
You forget the words he said:
I am with you to the end.
I am with you to the end.

Therefore watch and pray.
You know not the time.
He is coming with great power
when you least expect.
We repeat creation's plea:
Come, Lord Jesus, quickly come!
Come, Lord Jesus, quickly come!

From *Aleluya: Singing the Church Year*, by Corean Bakke

PART VI

DAILY READINGS AND PRAYERS

These daily readings focus on the stories that lead from season to season through the church year. They are not intended to be comprehensive, sophisticated, uniform, or texts for in-depth Bible study. Each is offered as a short, thought provoking, relevant reading that may contain a single idea to ponder throughout the day.

Most stories are spread over an entire week. When such a story does not have a plentiful supply of verses, a daily reading may be only one verse. Short readings function much as a continued story read aloud. They end with suspense, waiting for the next day. When stories may be too long for the length of time available, a shorter option is available in brackets.

These readings are designed for use by individuals and by family groups including children. The hope is that all the readings will provide nuggets for meditation throughout the day.

These undated daily readings require the reader to plan as each season progresses, using the calendar constructed on page 49. Keep in mind that these readings are selected as though every season begins and concludes with complete weeks. The church year is not that tidy.

Scripture references with accompanying titles are given for each week and each day. Maps are included for each season's readings. The prayers are deliberately brief so they can be easily memorized and used repeatedly.

The church year is like a book. The seasons are like chapters in that book, advancing the plot. The plot thickens. The worst happens. Jesus' followers are devastated. And then amazing things happen. The story continued in unforeseen ways.

It still continues and enfolds all those who wish to live in the story.

ADVENT READINGS AND PRAYER

ADVENT – Luke Chapter 1

Week I – Zechariah – 1-25
    Sunday   1-7   Priestly Couple   [5-7]
    Monday   8-10   Priest of the Day
    Tuesday   11-14   Angel
    Wednesday   15-17   Destiny
    Thursday   18-20   Unbelief
    Friday   21-22   Mute Priest
    Saturday   23-25   Pregnant Wife

Week II – Angel's Announcement – 26-45, 56
    Sunday   26-28   Gabriel
    Monday   29-33   Confusion
    Wednesday   34-38   Servant
    Thursday   39-40   Elizabeth
    Friday   41-42   Holy Spirit
    Saturday   43-45, 56   Question

Week III – Mary's Prayer – 46-55
    Sunday   46-49   Personal
    Monday   50   Mercy
    Tuesday   51   Power
    Wednesday   52   Control
    Thursday   53   Justice
    Friday   54   Helper
    Saturday   55   Promise

Week IV – John – 57-80
    Sunday   57-58   Birth
    Monday   59-60   Name
    Tuesday   61-63   Argument
    Wednesday   64-66   Fright
    Thursday   67-75   Savior   [67-69]
    Friday   76-79   Prophet   [76-77]
    Saturday   80   John

> Jesus
>
> Savior
> God
>
> You
> promised
> to come
>
> We wait
>
> Amen

CHRISTMAS READINGS AND PRAYER

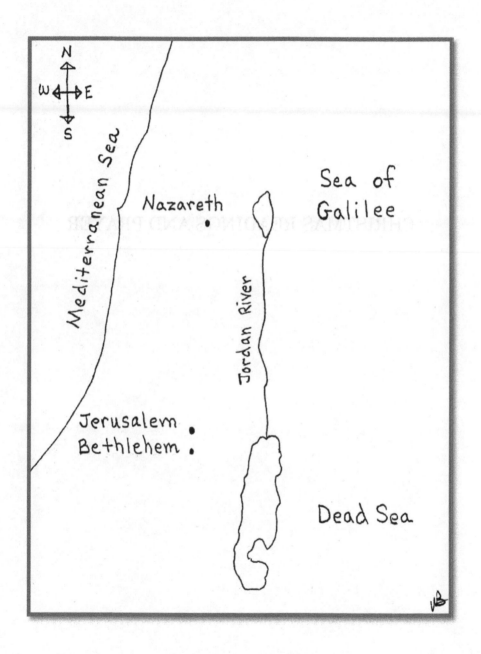

CHRISTMAS – Luke 2

Dec 25   Birth   1-7

Dec 26   Angels   8-14

Dec 27   Shepherds   15-20

Dec 28   Infant male ritual   21

Dec 29   Parental ritual   22-24

Dec 30   Simeon   25-28

Dec 31   Prayer   29-32

Jan 1   Blessing   33-35

Jan 2   Anna   36-38

Jan 3   Nazareth   39-40

Jan 4   Lost   41-47

Jan 5   Found   48-52

> Jesus
>
> We celebrate your coming
>
> God is with us
>
> Amen

EPIPHANY READINGS AND PRAYER

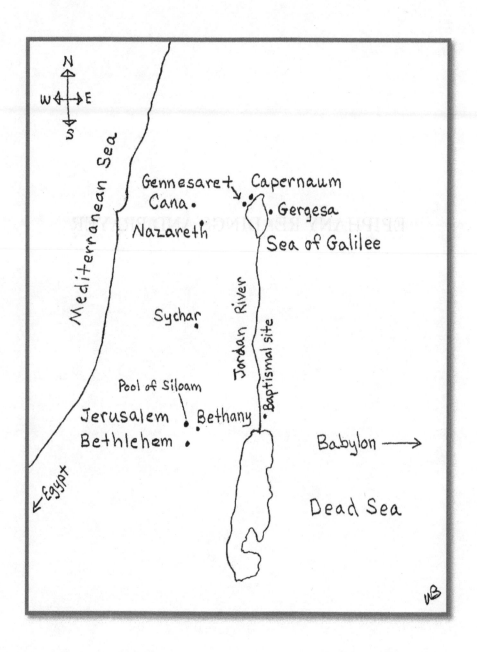

EPIPHANY

Week I – Wisemen – Matthew 2
    Sunday 1-2 Question
    Monday 3-6 King Herod
    Tuesday 7-8 Answer
    Wednesday 9-12 Success
    Thursday 13-15 Escape
    Friday 16-18 Massacre
    Saturday 19-23 Nazareth

Week II – Baptism – Matthew 3
    Sunday 1-2 John the Baptist
    Monday 3 Prophecy
    Tuesday 4-6 Description
    Wednesday 7-10 Sermon Part One [7-8]
    Thursday 11-12 Sermon Part Two [11]
    Friday 13-15 Jesus
    Saturday 16-17 Baptism

Week III – Wedding/Picnic – John 2 and 6
    Sunday 2:1-5 Mary
    Monday 2:6-8 Servants
    Tuesday 2:9-10 Wine
    Wednesday 2:11 Miracle
    Thursday 6:1-6 Test
    Friday 6:7-11 Food
    Saturday 6:12-15 Miracle

Week IV – Blind Man – John 9
    Sunday 1-7 Question
    Monday 8-12 Mud
    Tuesday 13-17 Interrogation
    Wednesday 18-23 Parents
    Thursday 24-29 More Interrogation
    Friday 30-34 Frustration
    Saturday 35-41 Belief [35-38]

Lord Jesus

Lighten the darkness

Show us the way

Amen

EPIPHANY

Week V – Samaritan Woman – John 4
    Sunday 3-10 Well
    Monday 11-14 Discussion
    Tuesday 15-19 Requests
    Wednesday 20-26 Messiah [25-26]
    Thursday 27-30 Surprises
    Friday 31-38 Food [31-35]
    Saturday 39-42 Belief

Week VI – Fish/Leper – Luke 5
    Sunday 1-3 Teaching
    Monday 4-5 Command
    Tuesday 6-7 Fish
    Wednesday 8-10a Result
    Thursday 10b-11 People
    Friday 12-14 Leper
    Saturday 15-16 News

Week VII – Demoniac – Luke 8
    Sunday 26-27 Man
    Monday 28-29 Demon
    Tuesday 30-31 Question
    Wednesday 32-33 Pigs
    Thursday 34-35c News
    Friday 35d-37a Fright
    Saturday 37b-39 Command

Week VIII – Lazarus – John 11
    Sunday 1-6 Sick Man
    Monday 17-19 Death
    Tuesday 20-27 Martha [20-22]
    Wednesday 28-31 Message
    Thursday 32-37 Mary
    Friday 38-42 Prayer
    Saturday 43-45 Jesus

> Lord Jesus
>
> Lighten the darkness
>
> Show us the way
>
> Amen

EPIPHANY

Last Week[19] – Crippled Man[20] – Mark 2
    Sunday 1-4 Crowd
    Monday 5-7 Forgiveness
    Tuesday 8-12 Amazement

Lord Jesus

Lighten the darkness

Show us the way

Amen

---

[19] Epiphany always ends with a partial week: Sunday, Monday, and Tuesday. Wednesday is Ash Wednesday, the beginning of Lent.

[20] The lectionary text for this Sunday is the Transfiguration, a story of Jesus alone with three of his disciples. John, one of those three, omitted that private occasion from his gospel. His stated goal was the selection of stories to persuade people to believe in Jesus. John 20:30-31

LENTEN READINGS AND PRAYER

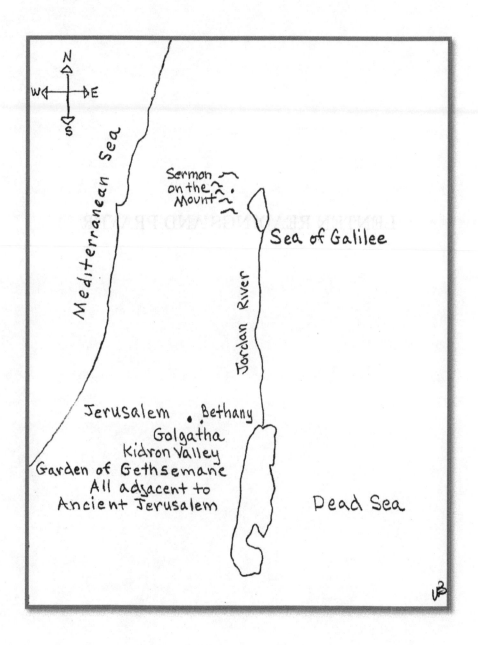

LENT

Ash Wednesday – Humankind – Genesis 2:7-8, 15-18, 21-23
Thursday – Sin – Genesis 3:1-7
Friday – Questions – Genesis 3:8-13
Saturday – Curse – Genesis 3:14, 16-17a, 19

Week I – Temptation – Matthew 4
    Sunday 1-2 Vulnerability
    Monday 3 Reputation
    Tuesday 4 Response
    Wednesday 5-6 Challenge
    Thursday 7 Response
    Friday 8-9 Gift
    Saturday 10-11 Response

Week II – Good Deeds – Matthew 6
    Sunday 1-4 Humbleness
    Monday 5-8 Privacy
    Tuesday 9-13 Prayer Pattern
    Wednesday 14-15 Forgiveness
    Thursday 16-18 Fasting Guidelines
    Friday 19-24 Treasure [19-21]
    Saturday 25-34 Worry [31-33]

Week III – Judging Others – Matthew 7
    Sunday 1-5 Self-critique
    Monday 6 Discrimination
    Tuesday 7-8 Promises
    Wednesday 9-11 Gifts
    Thursday 12 Golden Rule
    Friday 13-14 Narrow Gate
    Saturday 15-20 Good and Bad

> Lord
>
> Have mercy
>
> Forgive our sins
>
> Teach us forgiveness
>
> Amen

LENT

Week IV – Instructions – Matthew 10
   Sunday 16-20 Advice
   Monday 21-23 Hostility
   Tuesday 24-25 Status
   Wednesday 26-31 Confidence
   Thursday 32-33 Witness
   Friday 34-39 Trouble
   Saturday 40-42 Rewards

Week V – Predictions – Luke 21
   Sunday 5-6 Temple
   Monday 7-9 Impostors
   Tuesday 10-19 Signs
   Wednesday 20-24 Jerusalem
   Thursday 25-28 More Signs
   Friday 29-33 Meaning
   Saturday 34-38 Warning

Week VI – Passion – John's Gospel
   Sunday 12:1-7 Anointment
   Monday 12:12-19 Procession
   Tuesday 13:3-5, 12-17 Feet [3-5,15]
   Wednesday 13:33-35 Love
   Thursday 18:1-8 Garden
   Friday 18:28-30; 19:16-18, 28-30,
      38-42 Death and Burial
   Saturday I Peter 3:18b-20a Hell[21]

> Lord
>
> Have mercy
>
> Forgive our sins
>
> Teach us forgiveness
>
> Amen

---

[21] The Apostles' Creed, an ancient baptismal confession of faith used to this day by the Western church, includes, "He descended into hell." This belief about Jesus is based on I Peter 3:18-20 and Luke 23:43.

EASTER READINGS AND PRAYER

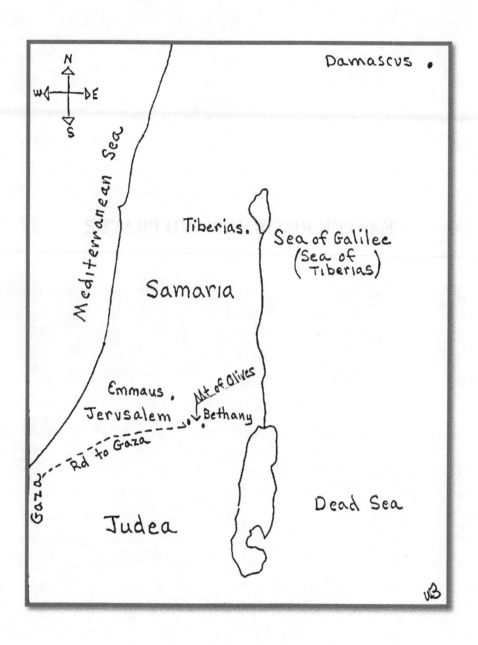

EASTER

Week I – Resurrection
    Sunday Luke 24:1-4a Tomb
    Monday Luke 24: 4b-8 Angels
    Tuesday Luke 24: 9-11 Report
    Wednesday Luke 24:12 Peter
    Thursday Matthew 28:11-15 Bribe
    Friday John 20:1-5 Discovery
    Saturday John 20: 6-10 Peter and John

Week II – Mary Magdalene – John 20
    Sunday 11-12 Angels
    Monday 13-14 Question
    Tuesday 15 Questions
    Wednesday 16 "Mary!"
    Thursday 17-18 Command
    Friday 19-20 Disciples
    Saturday 21-23 Holy Spirit

God

You amaze us

You always win!

Aleluya

Aleluya

Amen

Week III – Thomas – John 20
    Sunday 24-25a Absent
    Monday 25b Conditions
    Tuesday 26a-c Present
    Wednesday 26d-27 Command
    Thursday 28 Convinced
    Friday 29 Belief
    Saturday 30-31 John's Gospel

Week IV – Emmaus – Luke 24
    Sunday 13-16 Walk
    Monday 17-19a Questions
    Tuesday 19b-21 Crucifixion
    Wednesday 22-24 Body
    Thursday 25-27 Questions
    Friday 28-29 Invitation
    Saturday 30-32 Meal

EASTER

Week V – Jerusalem – Luke 24
    Sunday 33-35 Confirmation
    Monday 36-37 Fright
    Tuesday 38-39 Questions
    Wednesday 40-41a Proof
    Thursday 41b-43 Request
    Friday 44-48 Review
    Saturday 49 Wait

Week VI – Fishing – John 21
    Sunday 1-6 Advice
    Monday 7-11 Result
    Tuesday 12-14 Jesus
    Wednesday 15-17 Jesus' Question
    Thursday 18-19 Prediction
    Friday 20-22 Peter's Question
    Saturday 23-25 Clarification [23]

Week VII – Jesus Returns to Heaven – Acts 1
    Sunday 1-3 Introduction
    Monday 4-5 Wait
    Tuesday 6-8 Holy Spirit
    Wednesday 9-11 Ascension
    Thursday 12-14 Jerusalem
    Friday 15-20 Peter's Speech [15-19]
    Saturday 21-26 Matthias [21-22, 26]

God

You
amaze us

You
always
win!

Aleluya

Aleluya

Amen

PENTECOST READINGS AND PRAYERS

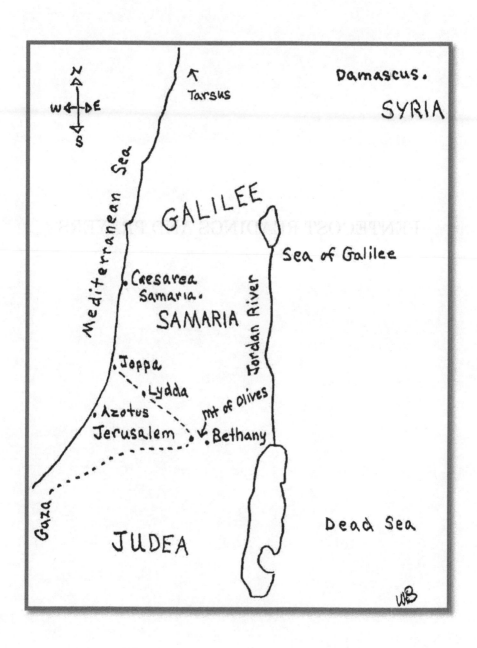

PENTECOST I

Weeks I – IX: Acts 2 – 10

Week I – Pentecost – Acts 2
     Sunday 1-13 Confusion [1-6, 12-13]
     Monday 14-21 Prophecy [14-18]
     Tuesday 22-28 Prophecy [22-24]
     Wednesday 29-31 David
     Thursday 32-36 Gift [32-33]
     Friday 37-42 Repentance
     Saturday 43-47 Believers

Week II – Lame Man – Acts 3
     Sunday 1-6 Gift
     Monday 7-10 Healed
     Tuesday 11-13 Sermon
     Wednesday 14-16 Faith
     Thursday 17-21 Repent
     Friday 22-23 Listen
     Saturday 24-26 Blessing

> Holy Spirit
>
> Helper within
>
> Grow us as you will
>
> Amen

Week III – Council – Acts 4
     Sunday 1-4 Arrested
     Monday 5-7 Question
     Tuesday 8-12 Jesus
     Wednesday 13-17 Strategy
     Thursday 18-22 Released
     Friday 23-28 Prayer
     Saturday 29-31 Request

PENTECOST I

Week IV – Good/Bad – Acts 4:32-5:42
    Sunday 4:32-37 Sharing
    Monday 5:1-11 Lies
    Tuesday 12-21a Miracles
    Wednesday 21b-28 Arrested
    Thursday 29-33 Response
    Friday 34-39a Gamaliel
    Saturday 39b-42 Whipped

Week V – Leaders – Acts 6
    Sunday 1 Complaint
    Monday 2-4 Solution
    Tuesday 5 Implementation
    Wednesday 6-7 Dedication
    Thursday 8-11 Opposition
    Friday 12-14 Mob
    Saturday 15-7:1 Council

Week VI – Stephen's Response – Acts 7
    Sunday 2-9a Ancestors [2-3]
    Monday 9b-19 Joseph [9b-10]
    Tuesday 20-39 Moses [20-22]
    Wednesday 40-47 Aaron [40-41]
    Thursday 48-50 God
    Friday 51-53 Stubborn!
    Saturday 54-60 Stoned

Week VII – Philip – Acts 8
    Sunday 1-3 Trouble
    Monday 4-8 Samaria
    Tuesday 9-25 Simon [11, 18-20, 22]
    Wednesday 26-28 Road to Gaza
    Thursday 29-31 Chariot
    Friday 32-35 Isaiah
    Saturday 36-40 Baptism

Holy Spirit

Helper
within

Grow us as
you will

Amen

174

PENTECOST I

Week VIII – Saul/Peter – Acts 9
     Sunday 1-9 Blinded [3-9]
     Monday 10-16 Ananias
     Tuesday 17-19a Healed
     Wednesday 19b-25 Damascus [19b-21]
     Thursday 26-31 Jerusalem [26-27]
     Friday 32-35 Aeneas
     Saturday 36-43 Dorcas [36-40]

Week IX – Cornelius – Acts 10
     Sunday 1-8 Vision in Caesarea
     Monday 9-16 Vision in Joppa
     Tuesday 17-23a Guests
     Wednesday 23b-29 Question
     Thursday 30-33 Cornelius
     Friday 34-43 Equality [34-35, 43]
     Saturday 44-48 Holy Spirit

Holy Spirit

Helper within

Grow us as you will

Amen

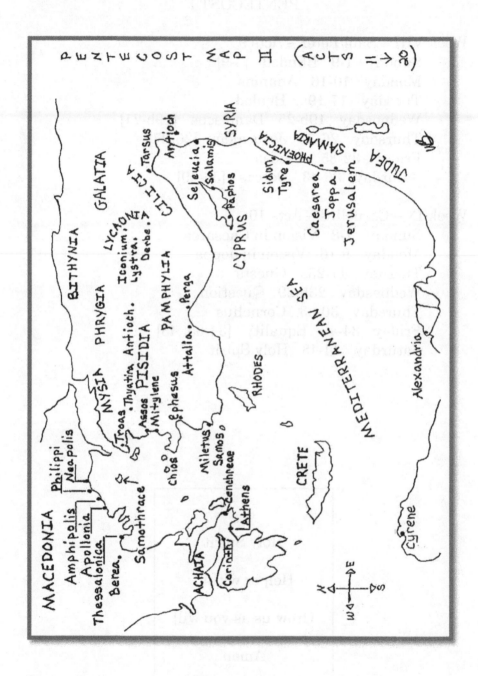

PENTECOST MAP II (ACTS 11 → 20)

PENTECOST II

Weeks X – XIX: Acts 11 – 20

Week X – Church Report – Acts 11
    Sunday 1-3 Argument
    Monday 4-10 Vision
    Tuesday 11-14 Trip
    Wednesday 15-18 Holy Spirit
    Thursday 19-22 Antioch
    Friday 23-26 Christians
    Saturday 27-30 Famine

Week XI – Herod – Acts 12
    Sunday 1-5 Herod
    Monday 6-9 Angel
    Tuesday 10-12 Rescued
    Wednesday 13-17 Rhoda
    Thursday 18-19 Soldiers
    Friday 20-23 Death
    Saturday 24-25 John Mark

> Holy Spirit
>
> Helper within
>
> Grow us as you will
>
> Amen

Week XII – First Journey Paul/Barnabas – Acts 13
    Sunday 1-3 Commissioning
    Monday 4-12 Cyprus [4-8, 12]
    Tuesday 13-14 Antioch
    Wednesday 15-37 Sermon [15-16, 32-33a]
    Thursday 38-43 Freedom
    Friday 44-48 Sabbath
    Saturday 49-52 Dust

PENTECOST II

Week XIII – First Journey Completed – Acts 14
    Sunday 1-3 Iconium
    Monday 4-7 Escape
    Tuesday 8-12 Lystra
    Wednesday 13-18 Sacrifice [13, 18]
    Thursday 19-20 Trouble
    Friday 21-23 Encouragement
    Saturday 24-28 Completion [25b-27]

Week XIV – Jerusalem – Acts 15
    Sunday 1-2 Problem
    Monday 3-5 Circumcision
    Tuesday 6-11 Peter
    Wednesday 12-21 James [19]
    Thursday 22-29 Letter [28]
    Friday 30-35 Delivered [30-31]
    Saturday 36-41 Separation [39-40]

Week XV – Second Journey Paul/Silas – Acts 16
    Sunday 1-5 Timothy
    Monday 6-10 Vision
    Tuesday 11-15 Lydia
    Wednesday 16-21 Accusation
    Thursday 22-28 Earthquake
    Friday 29-34 Jailer
    Saturday 35-40 Rights

Week XVI – Greek Cities – Acts 17
    Sunday 1-4 Thessalonica
    Monday 5-9 Jealousy
    Tuesday 10-15 Berea
    Wednesday 16-18 Athens
    Thursday 19-23 Areopagus
    Friday 24-31 Explanation [24-25, 31]
    Saturday 32-34 Ridicule/Belief

> Holy
> Spirit
>
> Helper
> within
>
> Grow us
> as you
> will
>
> Amen

PENTECOST II

Week XVII – Second Journey Completed
        Third Begun – Acts 18
    Sunday   1-3   Corinth
    Monday   4-6   Insult
    Tuesday   7-11   Vision   [9-10]
    Wednesday   12-13   Court
    Thursday   14-17   Gallio   [14-15]
    Friday   18-23   Travels   [18]
    Saturday   24-28   Apollos   [24-26]

Week XVIII – Ephesus – Acts 19
    Sunday   1-7   Ephesus   [1, 6]
    Monday   8-10   Speaking   [10]
    Tuesday   11-20   Miracles   [11-12, 20]
    Wednesday   21-27   Silversmith   [24-27]
    Thursday   28-29   Riot
    Friday   30-34   Paul   [30-31]
    Saturday   35-41   Town Official   [35-36]

Week XIX – Farewells – Acts 20
    Sunday   1-6   Travels   [2-3a]
    Monday   7-9   Fall
    Tuesday   10-12   Eutychus
    Wednesday   13-16   Voyage   [16]
    Thursday   17-24   Meeting   [24]
    Friday   25-31   Task Completed   [27-28a]
    Saturday   32-38   Farewells   [32a, 36-38]

> Holy
> Spirit
>
> Helper
> within
>
> Grow us
> as you
> will
>
> Amen

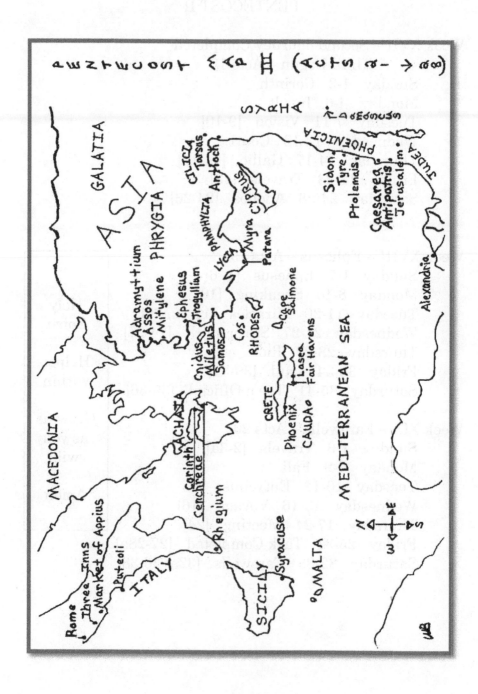

PENTECOST III

Weeks XX – XXVII: Acts 21 – 28
Final Week – Christ the King – Matthew 25

Week XX – Third Journey Completed – Acts 21
Sunday   1-9   Voyage
Monday   10-13   Warning
Tuesday   14-16   Onward   [14]
Wednesday   17-26   Predicament   [19-21]
Thursday   27-29   Agitators
Friday   30-36   Riot
Saturday   37-40   Commander

Week XXI – Paul's Defense – Acts 22
Sunday   1-3   Quiet
Monday   4-5   Trouble-maker
Tuesday   6-11   Bright light
Wednesday   12-16   Ananias
Thursday   17-20   Vision
Friday   21-23   Riot Resumed
Saturday   24-30   Roman Citizen   [24-25, 29]

Week XXII – Trauma – Acts 23
Sunday   1-5   High Priest
Monday   6-9   Fierce Argument
Tuesday   10-11   Assurance
Wednesday   12-15   Plot
Thursday   16-22   Nephew
Friday   23-33   Security
Saturday   34   Governor

> Holy Spirit
>
> Helper within
>
> Grow us as you will
>
> Amen

PENTECOST III

Week XXIII – Court – Acts 24
  Sunday 1-9 Lawyer
  Monday 10-16 Defense
  Tuesday 17-21 Charge
  Wednesday 22 Governor
  Thursday 23 Lenient Guard
  Friday 24-26 Audience
  Saturday 27 Not Released

Week XXIV – Appeal to Rome – Acts 25
  Sunday 1-5 Maneuver
  Monday 6-7 Court
  Tuesday 8-9 Defense
  Wednesday 10-11 Appeal
  Thursday 12 Success
  Friday 13-22 Agrippa and Bernice [13-14, 22]
  Saturday 23-27 Festus' Plan

Week XXV – Paul's Defense – Acts 26
  Sunday 1-8 Religion [2-3]
  Monday 9-11 Opposition
  Tuesday 12-18 Confrontation [12-16]
  Wednesday 19-23 Obedience [19-20]
  Thursday 24-26 Crazy!
  Friday 27-29 Questions
  Saturday 30-32 Conclusion

Week XXVI – Voyage – Acts 27
  Sunday 1-12 Problems [1, 7-11]
  Monday 13-20 Storm [18-20]
  Tuesday 21-26 Paul [23-26]
  Wednesday 27-29 Danger
  Thursday 30-32 Sailors
  Friday 33-38 Food
  Saturday 39-44 Shipwreck

Holy Spirit

Helper within

Grow us as
you will

Amen

PENTECOST III

Week XXVII – Voyage Concludes – Acts 28
      Sunday 1-2 Malta
      Monday 3-6 Snake
      Tuesday 7-10 Welcome
      Wednesday 11-15 Another Ship
      Thursday 16-22 Rome [16]
      Friday 23-29 Jews Leave [28-29]
      Saturday 30-31 House

Last Week – The Final Judgment – Matthew 25

    Reading for Christ the King Sunday
        and week following

      Sunday 31-33 All People
      Monday 34-36 Sheep
      Tuesday 37-39 Question
      Wednesday 40 Answer
      Thursday 41-43 Goats
      Friday 44 Question
      Saturday 45-46 Answer

> Come
>
> Lord Jesus
>
> Quickly come
>
> Amen

AFTERWORD

Spirituality is that which nourishes the inner life.

The personal spirituality described here has evolved layer by layer. It began with the daily scripture readings and prayer in my parents' home. It expanded into a quest for tradition in corporate worship. Classroom lectures and assignments led to unexplored models and perspectives. A move to the Pacific Northwest added a surprising dimension.

The church year, an ancient tradition creaking with age, has emerged with fresh and relevant meaning for the seasons of contemporary living.

Naming Advent as the season of expectation – a time of waiting – lifted the burden of frantic preparations for Christmas. I enjoy these four weeks as never before.

With twelve days to celebrate Christmas, I no longer feel compelled to cram the schedule full before December 25. Festivities with family and friends are spread throughout those days.

Epiphany has been the most challenging season to personalize. Unwilling to describe it using a word more suited to a cross-word puzzle than everyday conversation,[22] I searched for a word that was part of my day-to-day life and needed no definition. Practicing the season required a clear descriptive word. *Discovery* removed the frustration, enabling me to write an Epiphany hymn and select daily scripture readings. As for the color *orange*, it beautifully complements our terra-cotta floor tiles.

---

[22] See word *manifestation* on page 41.

Thinking of Lent as a time of testing supports me during hard times and provides a context for responding to the hard times of others. Jesus promised that we would be tested and that he would be with us through it all to the end of our lives.

After years of Easter celebrations significantly overshadowed by Christmas celebrations, I was excited to become part of a church tradition that expanded the observance of Easter. Ever since my first experience of *Triduum* – the three-part/three-day service of Maundy Thursday, Good Friday, and the Vigil of Easter – when I participated in an elaborate arrival to the most important feast day of Christendom, I have looked for ways to enhance Easter.

In Mark's Gospel, when three women found the tomb empty, they were amazed. I named this the season of amazement. God wins over the Devil's seeming success in getting rid of Jesus.

Pentecost now has relevance for me. Growing into new skills takes time. Six months is not too long. I am a project person and never lack for things to occupy my time. But I often get in over my head and need help. I depend on the Spirit to guide, teach, and empower me to finish things that I start and steer me away from things I should avoid. I need to be kept on course as I follow Jesus.

With this personal narrative of living an ancient tradition, I conclude my description of the church year, my adaptation of it, and the practices in my home. A simple request has become a book.

BIBLIOGRAPHY

Adam, Adolf. *The Liturgical Year: Its History and Its Meaning After the Reform of the Liturgy.* Trans. Matthew J. O'Connell. New York: Pueblo Publishing Company, 1981.

Bailey, Albert Edward. *The Gospel in Hymns: Backgrounds and Interpretations.* New York: Charles Schribner's Sons, 1950.

Bell, John, and Graham Maule. *Wild Goose Songs,* Vol 1: Songs of Creation, the Incarnation, and the Life of Jesus. Glasgow: Wild Goose Publications, 1987.

Black, Vicki K. *Welcome to the Church Year: An Introduction to the Seasons of the Episcopal Church.* Harrisburg: Morehouse Publishing, 2004.

Boling, Ruth, illustrated by Tracey Dahle Carrier. *Come Worship With Me: A Journey through the Church Year.* Louisville: Geneva Press, 2001.

The Book of Common Prayer. New York: The Church Hymnal Corporation, 1979.

Broderick, Robert C. *The Catholic Encyclopedia.* Nashville: Thomas Nelson Inc., Publishers, 1976.

Buckland, Patricia B. *Advent to Pentecost: A History of the Christian Year.* Wilton, Conn.: Morehouse-Barlow Co., Inc., 1979.

Cowie, L.W., and John Selwyn Gummer. *The Christian Calendar: A Complete Guide to the Seasons of the Christian Year Telling the Story of Christ and the Saints from Advent to Pentecost*. Springfield, Mass.: G & C Merriam Company, Publishers, 1974.

Davis, Moshe, and Isaac Levy. *Journeys of the Children of Israel*. 2nd ed. rev. London: Thomas Nelson (Printers) Ltd, 1967.

Davies, J.G., ed. *A Dictionary of Liturgy and Worship*. New York: The Macmillan Company, 1972.

Emmert, Martha Atkins. *Common Clay*. Fort Wayne: Martha Atkins Emmert, 1997.

Evangelical Lutheran Worship. Minneapolis: Augsburg Fortress, 2006.

Favorite Songs and Hymns: A Complete Church Hymnal. Dallas: Stamps-Baxter Music & Printing Co., Inc., 1939.

Gorney, Cynthia. 2011. "A People Apart" (http://ngm.nationalgeographic.com/2008/11/tarahumara-people/gorney-text).

The Good News: The New Testament with Over 500 Illustrations and Maps. New York: The American Bible Society, segments copyrighted in 1951, 1953, and 1955.

Good News Bible: The Bible In Today's English Version. New York: American Bible Society, 1976.

Gross, Bobby. *Living the Christian Year: Time To Inhabit the Story Of God*. Downers Grove, Ill.: IVP Books (an imprint of InterVarsity Press), 2009.

Gwynne, Walker. *The Christian Year: Its Purpose and Its History*. New York: Longmans, Green, and Co., 1917. Reprinted in Detroit: Grand River Books, 1971.

Holy Bible: Contemporary English Version. New York: American Bible Society, 1995.

Ireton, Kimberlee Conway. *The Circle of Seasons: Meeting God in the Church Year*. Downers Grove, Ill.: IVP Books (an Imprint of InterVarsity Press), 2008.

Jones, Cheslyn, Geoffrey Wainwright, and Edward Yarnold, eds. *The Study of Spirituality*. New York, Oxford: Oxford University Press, 1986.

Liturgy: The Christmas Cycle. Volume 9, Number 3, 1991. Journal of The Liturgical Conference.

Liturgy: In Daily Life. Volume 7, Number 3, 1988. Journal of the Liturgical Conference.

Lutheran Book of Worship. Minneapolis: Augsburg Publishing House, 1987.

Manual on the Liturgy: Lutheran Book of Worship. Minneapolis: Augsburg Fortress Publishing House, 1979.

May, Herbert G., ed. *Oxford Bible Atlas*. 2nd ed. London: Oxford University Press, 1976.

Nelson, Gertrud Mueller. *To Dance With God: Family and Community Celebration*. New York: Paulist Press, 1986.

Our Daily Bread: For Personal and Family Devotions. Dec – Feb 2010/2011. Grand Rapids: RBC Ministries, Radio Bible Class.

Peterson, Eugene H., ed. *Stories for the Christian Year* (The Chrysostom Society). New York: Macmillan Publishing Company, 1992.

Pfeiffer, Charles F. *Baker's Bible Atlas*. Grand Rapids: Baker Book House, 1961.

Rich, Tracey R. 2011. "Judaism 101" (http://www.jewfaq.org/index.htm).

Rochelle, Jay C. *The Revolutionary Year: Recapturing the Meaning of the Church Year*. Philadelphia: Fortress Press, 1973.

Senn, Frank C. *Christian Liturgy: Catholic and Evangelical*. Minneapolis: Fortress Press, 1997.

Spink, Kathryn, ed. *Life In The Spirit: Reflections, Meditations, Prayers: Mother Teresa of Calcutta*. San Francisco: Harper & Row, Publishers, 1983.

Todd, Galbraith Hall. *The Torch and The Flag*. Philadelphia: American Sunday-School Union, 1966.

The United Methodist Book of Worship. Nashville: The United Methodist Publishing House, 1992.

The Upper Room: Daily Devotional Guide. January-February 2011. Nashville: Upper Room Ministries.

Webber, Robert, compiler. *The Book of Daily Prayer*. Grand Rapids: Wm. B. Eerdmans Publishing Co., 1993.

Wikipedia. 2011. "Advent" (http://en.wikipedia.org/wiki/Advent).

Wikipedia. 2011. "Christmas"
(http://en.wikipedia.org/wiki/Christmas).

Wikipedia. 2011. "Epiphany"
(http://en.wikipedia.org/wiki/Epiphany).
Wikipedia. 2011. "Lent" (http://en.wikipedia.org/wiki/Lent).

Wikipedia. 2011. "Easter"
(http://en.wikipedia.org/wiki/Easter).

Wikipedia. 2011. "Pentecost"
(http://en.wikipedia.org/wiki/Pentecost).

Wilson, Frank E. *An Outline of The Christian Year*. New York: Morehouse-Gorham Co., 1944.

With One Voice: A Lutheran Resource for Worship. Minneapolis: Augsburg Fortress, 1995.

The Word In Season: Daily Devotions. Volume 78, Number 1. Minneapolis: Augsburg Fortress, 2010.

Corean and her husband Ray live at Bakken where she divides her time between music, writing, designing worship, hosting, and maintaining her home and gardens.

OTHER TITLES

Let the Whole World Sing (1994)

Aleluya: Singing the Church Year (2010)

Aleluya: The Music of Lausanne II – editor (1989, 1994)

Aleluya: The Songs of Renewal – co-editor (1992)

Time to Talk in Church About HIV and AIDS: A Bible Study Discussion Guide – co-author (2004), Russian translation (2008)